MW00377847

Praise for
Building Character with True Stories from Nature

"Lewis introduces fascinating aspects of the natural world—its constructive and destructive power—to young students in a way that reaches beyond knowledge acquisition. She shows teachers how to build bridges to the inner worlds of children with analogical thinking, reflective questions, and thoughtful conversations that nourish not only their understanding but their agency. If you want to use learning as a way to develop your students' character, intrinsic motivation, and an ethically grounded relationship with the world, this is the guide you need."

—*Diane Stirling, professional development coordinator for CHARACTERplus® and coauthor of* **Character Education Connections for School, Home, and Community**

"Barbara Lewis weaves factual information with down-to-earth, applicable activities and discussions to encourage students' appreciation for nature, while building their power to observe and to understand people and their world as multidimensional. Throughout, Lewis is respectful of children's capacity to discuss important issues and form their own opinions."

—*Silvia Blitzer Golombek, Ph.D., senior vice president, Youth Service America*

"Another delightful book from Barbara Lewis, *Building Character with True Stories from Nature* is filled with fascinating depictions and insightful analogies to support character development. We recommend Barbara Lewis's books to all the families who seek our services. Believing that children *can* make a difference, Lewis provides the inspiration for helping others, taking a stand against injustice, squelching rumors, and seeing beyond stereotypes. This book should be a staple in every school's social-emotional learning curriculum."

—*Linda Kreger Silverman, Ph.D., licensed psychologist, director of the Gifted Development Center*

"Creatively weds character education with analogies from nature to help teachers promote both deep learning and positive character development in students . . . this synergy is just what education should be."

—*Marvin W. Berkowitz, Ph.D., director, Sanford N. McDonnell Leadership Academy for Character Education for School Principals*

Building Character with True Stories from Nature

Barbara A. Lewis

free spirit
PUBLISHING®

Text copyright © 2012 by Barbara A. Lewis
Illustrations copyright © 2012 by Free Spirit Publishing Inc.

All rights reserved under International and Pan-American Copyright Conventions. Unless otherwise noted, no part of this book may be reproduced, stored in a retrieval system, or transmitted in any form or by any means, electronic, mechanical, photocopying, or otherwise, without express written permission of the publisher, except for brief quotations or critical reviews. For more information, go to www.freespirit.com/company/permissions.cfm.

Free Spirit, Free Spirit Publishing, and associated logos are trademarks and/or registered trademarks of Free Spirit Publishing Inc. A complete listing of our logos and trademarks is available at www.freespirit.com.

Library of Congress Cataloging-in-Publication Data
Lewis, Barbara A., 1943–
  Building character with true stories from nature / by Barbara A. Lewis.
    p. cm.
  Includes bibliographical references and index.
  ISBN 978-1-57542-418-7 — ISBN 1-57542-418-5
  1. Moral education. 2. Character—Study and teaching—Activity programs. 3. Nature study—Activity programs. 4. Animal ecology—Study and teaching. I. Title.
  LC268.L465 2012
  370.114—dc23   2012024391

eBook ISBN: 978-1-57542-650-1

Free Spirit Publishing does not have control over or assume responsibility for author or third-party websites and their content. At the time of this book's publication, all facts and figures cited within are the most current available. All telephone numbers, addresses, and website URLs are accurate and active; all publications, organizations, websites, and other resources exist as described in this book; and all have been verified as of June 2012. If you find an error or believe that a resource listed here is not as described, please contact Free Spirit Publishing. Parents, teachers, and other adults: We strongly urge you to monitor children's use of the Internet.

Photo credits: Page i (apple) © Inna Yurkevych | Dreamstime.com, (leaves) © Dmires | Dreamstime.com • **Page 14** © Curioustiger | Dreamstime.com • **Page 20** © Donkeyru | Dreamstime.com • **Page 25** © Azgek | Dreamstime.com • **Page 29** © Tomoki1970 | Dreamstime.com • **Page 34** © Onefivenine | Dreamstime.com • **Page 40** © Rainer von Brandis | istockphoto.com • **Page 45** © Thefinalmiracle | Dreamstime.com • **Page 51** © Melvinlee | Dreamstime.com • **Page 56** © Nemeziyaa | Dreamstime.com • **Page 62** © Cammeraydave | Dreamstime.com • **Page 68** © Honkamaa | Dreamstime.com • **Page 74** © Photoinmind | Dreamstime.com • **Page 80** © Nightowlza | Dreamstime.com • **Page 86** © Fergregory | Dreamstime.com • **Page 92** © Taiga | Dreamstime.com • **Page 98** © by CharlesLam (www.flickr.com/photos/kclama/3639316789/) [CC-BY-SA-2.0 (http://creativecommons.org/licenses/by-sa/2.0)], via Wikimedia Commons • **Page 103** © Mike_kiev | Dreamstime.com • **Page 109** © Matthias33 | Dreamstime.com • **Page 115** © Bernardbreton | Dreamstime.com • **Page 121** © Martinedegraaf | Dreamstime.com • **Page 127** © Raphoto | Dreamstime.com • **Page 133** © Imaginator | Dreamstime.com • **Page 139** © Lightwriter1949 | Dreamstime.com • **Page 145** © Mlane | Dreamstime.com • **Page 151** © Jianchun | Dreamstime.com

Edited by Alison Behnke
Cover and interior design by Tasha Kenyon

10 9 8 7 6 5 4 3 2 1
Printed in the United States of America

Free Spirit Publishing Inc.
Minneapolis, MN
(612) 338-2068
help4kids@freespirit.com
www.freespirit.com

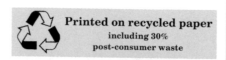

Printed on recycled paper
including 30%
post-consumer waste

As a member of the Green Press Initiative, Free Spirit Publishing is committed to the three Rs: Reduce, Reuse, Recycle. Whenever possible, we print our books on recycled paper containing a minimum of 30% post-consumer waste. At Free Spirit it's our goal to nurture not only children, but nature too!

green press INITIATIVE

Free Spirit offers competitive pricing.
Contact edsales@freespirit.com for pricing information on multiple quantity purchases.

Dedication

To my grandchildren, who still see the magic of nature:
Adam, Anderson, Andrew, Chloe, Clara, Houston, Jordan, Lizzie, Maddy, and Ruby

Acknowledgments

A special thanks to my publisher, Judy Galbraith, for her continued confidence in my work and her belief that good books can inspire the lives of kids. And a special thank you to Alison Behnke, who provided great guidance and outstanding editing. Thanks to all the Free Spirit Publishing team for their efforts in producing this book. I must recognize the Character Education Partnership, which continues to provide a proven path for the development of positive character traits—along with the many national organizations dedicated to developing character among young people. And thanks to Dr. Marvin Berkowitz for his wise advice and great example of what good character education should be.

Always, I thank my dear husband and best friend, Lawrence, for his love and support in this endeavor.

Contents

Note: Photos of each plant and animal are included on the CD-ROM.

Introduction

"And I cherish more than anything else the Analogies, my most trustworthy masters. They know all the secrets of Nature, and they ought to be least neglected."

—Mathematician and astronomer Johannes Kepler (1571–1630)

As a teacher, you've probably had the thrill of witnessing a student experience one of those "aha" moments, when something that was puzzling suddenly becomes clear. You've likely had more than a few of these moments yourself. And sometimes, something even more amazing happens. Sometimes, that aha moment can lead to a deeper understanding of character and an embracing of better choices and better positive habits.

It's tough to force such a transformation. But that doesn't mean that there aren't ways to prepare for it and even help it along. One of the greatest ways to set the stage for meaningful realization and positive change is through analogies. Analogical thinking—especially when practiced through interesting stories—fits naturally with character education. It actively engages kids in critical thinking and can also tap into their emotional responses. When these two experiences come together, the possibilities for learning and growth are enormous.

In your work with kids in grades 2 through 5, you have the chance to make a big difference. You can help shape the kinds of people your young students become. *Building Character with True Stories from Nature* gives you simple, effective ways to teach kids positive character traits and build healthful habits using powerful analogies and fascinating true stories from the natural world.

Creating Good Habits in the Brain

What makes analogies so effective? The answer lies in the way our brains work—right down to their cells.

From the moment of birth, the human brain is ready to respond to life by instantly making connections. Infants are born with about 100 billion neurons. These neurons are woven into enormous networks of communication, building the basic architecture of the brain. As kids grow, their brains are constantly making new connections and forming new neurons. Neurons send messages down axons, fibers that end in tree-like branches that reach out and connect with other neurons.

This remarkable growth and connection-making never stops. The human brain continues to adapt to new events, rewire itself, and grow new neurons throughout life. But development is most rapid and intense before adolescence. This is when kids can most easily learn new languages, math, music, athletic skills, and more. It's also when many kids form behavior patterns and build character traits, positive or otherwise.

Understanding the brain's connection-making process is important in helping your students develop strong character and good habits. Habits and behavior patterns are worn into the brain like often-used paths. When any behavior or thought pattern is repeated frequently enough, the brain's neurons create a pathway—and a habit. Over time, the habit seems easier and more natural. And it's tough to change. Even if a student doesn't always *want* to follow the neural pathway toward a certain action or thought pattern, he or she may feel pulled along it over and over again.

Because analogical thinking develops new neurons and connections, it's an efficient method of building these neural pathways. As your students revisit analogies and reconsider stories about good character, they create and strengthen their mental pathways, thereby creating and strengthening positive habits of thought. This process can also be described using an analogy:

Have you ever watched children make a sled run in the snow? If the hill isn't very steep, they first have to make the snow slick enough so that the sleds will slide down easily. Otherwise, they'll just be stuck in the snow. So kids pull their sleds down the same path over and over again. Eventually, the repeated process creates a slippery surface for sledding.

In the brain, when a student is reminded through stories and experience of positive character traits and actions, he or she is priming the pathways between neurons, causing the connections to happen more quickly and easily. Behavior and ways of thinking will change with time and practice. Teaching with analogical stories is one way of helping your students develop and prime these mental pathways to good habits.

Learning Through Analogies

Teachers have long known that analogies can help students understand new or difficult concepts. An analogy builds a bridge between the familiar and the unfamiliar. For example, a science teacher might compare a solar system (familiar information) to a tiny atom (new concept) to help students better understand atomic structure.

Analogical reasoning is also used to teach mathematics and problem solving. Language arts teachers explore analogies through poetry and other creative writing. Teachers in social studies, history, music, art, and sports also make use of analogies. Consider some of the exciting benefits of teaching with analogies:

Analogies increase cognitive growth and abilities. The brain is very adaptive. It grows new neurons when it's introduced to new and challenging activities and thoughts. And the creation of neurons and the connections between them occurs rapidly through childhood. Analogies are an excellent way to stimulate and support that growth.

Analogies develop higher-level thinking skills. Analogy is a form of inductive reasoning, leading students from specific observations to broader ideas. For example, if someone says that a friend is "like a rock" (a specific thing), then that friend is probably trustworthy and reliable (a broader idea). With analogies' power to develop and strengthen critical thinking, creativity, and other valuable skills, analogies are as important to teachers today as they've ever been.

Since the mid-1900s, cognitive researchers have recognized that analogies are basic to human thinking, and that they stimulate mental leaps of understanding. Using advanced brain scanning techniques such as the functional MRI, researchers have verified that analogical thinking involves the frontopolar regions of the brain. Analogies require the brain to be active in order to make connections between the familiar symbol and the unfamiliar target.

Research has also shown that children as young as three years old can understand simple analogies, as long as the child is familiar with the first object. Even thirteen-month-olds can begin to transfer information and learn by comparison. Understanding analogies may be a major milestone for children to achieve in the first year of life. In fact, many researchers believe that analogy is the primary means by which cognition develops.

In addition, analogies encourage an active, personal response. When receiving information from a teacher, it's all too easy for a learner to stop there—to simply receive the information passively and take the process no further. But an analogy requires at least three separate but related active responses, all of which incorporate higher-order thinking skills:

- *Participation.* The brain must be active and engaged to form connections between neurons. This active participation takes place with the analysis of the analogy.

- *Interpretation.* The brain must make sense out of the comparison.

- *Application.* The brain will make a personal response as to how the comparison might apply to the learner's experiences or those of others. For example, the lesson about ancient bristlecone pine trees (page 29) draws an analogy to inner strength. To a struggling student, that might mean overcoming an academic challenge. To an athlete, it might mean being a strong and able defender on the football field. To a person whose values have been challenged, it might mean standing up for his or her personal convictions.

Analogies can bring discovery and excitement to learning. Many kids find analogies more interesting and fun than scripted lectures or other lesson formats. When teaching about positive character traits, you might want your students to think about taking personal responsibility for their own actions instead of blaming others. Talking about these traits and behaviors is valuable. Using the analogy of the crow that attacks its own reflection (page 46) will add even more life to your lesson, providing an exciting moment of discovery as kids grasp connections between the story and their own lives.

Analogies can be time-savers. They transfer details and understanding from something familiar to a new topic. They are also time-savers because, once familiar with them, you can use them when you need them, without much preparation or planning. For example, if two of your students are having a disagreement or argument, you might quickly revisit the story of rapidly growing bamboo (page 21) in helping them think about the way disagreements can grow and escalate. The bamboo story can bring a pause to the argument and provide common, neutral ground for a productive discussion. The kids may then be in a better frame of mind to draw connections between the story and their situation, and to discuss solutions.

Analogies help students remember what they've learned. Analogies capture the creative mind's attention. They invite students to imagine visual representations of abstract concepts. Recalling this visual representation can be a helpful memory tool.

Analogies are useful learning tools for students with a wide range of abilities and needs. Analogies help students build on prior knowledge and make sense of the complex or unfamiliar. They also improve their ability to see patterns.

Strong analogies can create emotional responses. Kids might laugh, feel happy or sad, or even get angry when they grasp certain comparisons. Behavior improvement is most effective when learners are intensely engaged and also feel emotion. Strong analogical stories can stimulate both of these reactions in the brain.

Powerful analogies can motivate action or inspire changes in behavior. Analogies stimulate interest, enticing kids to find out more. They're then motivated to explore this new knowledge and to experiment with it. For example, when students read about quaking aspens (page 128) and learn their secret of connectedness, they may be inspired to seek better

support and connections in their families, friendships, classmates, or teams. This aspect of analogical thinking, in particular, makes *Building Character with True Stories from Nature* special. When you combine the power of analogies with character education, amazing things can happen.

Building Positive Character Habits with Analogies

We've all heard the old adage that habits are easy to make but hard to break. Developing positive habits—and staying away from unwanted ones—can be a lifelong effort. It takes strong character "muscles." Just like any other muscle, character muscles grow strong through use. The more a student practices kindness and caring, for example, the easier it becomes. You can help your students develop their character muscles by using true stories and analogies that create positive pathways in the brain. For example, if you want to encourage truthfulness from your students (or if honesty is an issue in your classroom), simply discussing the importance of honesty or even demanding it won't ensure positive habits or changes in behavior. Instead, character building

Scientific studies have demonstrated strong connections between analogies and learning. In one study, various scientific concepts were taught to students in grades 3 through 6. In the first experiment, some students read lessons that incorporated analogies, while others read texts that did not use analogies. When asked to recall the lessons and to answer questions, students who had read the analogical texts showed higher levels of performance than those who had read non-analogical texts. In a second experiment, texts were read aloud to students in grades 3 and 5. The texts *with* analogies were read only once. The texts *lacking* analogies were read twice. Just as in the first experiment, students who heard the analogies demonstrated better reasoning than those who did not, even though they had spent less time with the texts.

and thought patterns must begin in the brain—and the process takes time. Several main steps comprise this process.

Ignoring an old pathway by not using it. Suppose Anthony has a sweet tooth and wants to develop the positive habit of eating more healthful foods. Reading the story of the unfortunate turkey that is too heavy to fly (page 139), he starts to think about whether he's willing to lose the ability to fly—figuratively speaking. Each time he gets the urge for a candy bar or a cookie, he resists. He reminds himself of the story. He thinks through his choices and the consequences of each, and he snacks on some carrot sticks or an apple instead. When the craving strikes again, he remembers the turkey again, and so on. Over time, as Anthony repeatedly responds to sugar cravings by eating nutritious foods, he starts to develop a new neural pathway. He won't stop craving sweets all at once, but the sugar-craving pathway in his brain weakens and breaks down over time as he stops following it. Symbolically, the neglected path grows weeds.

Building a new pathway. At the same time that Anthony stops taking the old habit pathway, he's also taking additional steps to build a new pathway. He can continue to remind himself of the story of the turkey. Meanwhile, he takes action by throwing away the candy he has stashed in his desk. He stops taking cookies in his lunch. And he continues to replace the urge for sweets by eating nuts, vegetables, and other wholesome foods. As he repeats these positive actions, Anthony creates a new neural pathway toward better habits.

Priming the new pathway through repetition. Developing or changing a habitual behavior requires repetition. As Anthony continues to repeat his new behavior habits, his brain gets accustomed to the new path. He starts to enjoy eating more healthful food. He begins to crave the taste of fruits and veggies. He will have created a new habit channel in his brain. Remember the sledding hill analogy? The kids don't create the slick hill by sledding down just once. The process requires repeated sledding. Likewise, one analogy from nature can motivate someone to work toward a character goal or a positive behavior, but well-established habits and long-term change require repeated reminders and experiences.

Why Use True Stories from Nature?

Stories and analogies from nature provide fun starting points for character-focused discussion. Most kids respond with interest and enthusiasm to stories of animals and plants. In addition, drawing analogies to these objects from nature rather than making comparisons between people is a safe and nonthreatening way to explore character without getting too personal or appearing to judge, criticize, or praise specific individuals. For example, if you compare two students—Sasha, who almost always remembers to do her homework—with Nick, who can't seem to remember to bring his assignments home—Nick is likely to feel embarrassed and hurt, even if he doesn't show these feelings. He may also feel resentment toward Sasha. In fact, Nick will probably develop more resentment than dependability. He might feel attacked or view the comparison as unfair. Nick's thought process can get sidetracked by his resentment, hurt feelings, and anger. Meanwhile, your comparison gets ignored, and an opportunity for positive character building may be lost.

Nature, however, remains a safe distance from human behavior. If you read to your group the story about dogs (page 63), Nick can understand and accept the dependability of a dog without feeling threatened by it. He may even find the story emotionally moving or resonant. In the process, his brain can use the message to begin building a new neuron pathway toward becoming more dependable. From the story, Nick can gain motivation and a deeper understanding of character.

Making Analogies Work for You

While analogies may incorporate metaphors and similes, they are more extended and complex than either of these concepts. An analogy is a logical argument that presents a parallel relationship between two words or ideas. Analogies show how two things are alike by pointing out the characteristics that they share, with the intent of showing that if two things are similar in some ways, they are also similar in other ways.

One half of any analogy is the familiar object, and the other half is the target concept to be explained. When creating analogies between nature and character, you can begin by choosing the familiar object of nature and also choosing a target concept related to human character traits and behavior. For example, you might choose a cat as the familiar object, and choose as your target concept the idea that curiosity without caution can sometimes get people into trouble.

Next, draw a general connection between the familiar object and the target concept. In this case, you can explore the well-known phenomenon that cats sometimes climb trees and are afraid to come back down. Through this idea, you can lead your group toward an understanding of the fact that people, too, can get themselves into frightening or dangerous situations.

The third step is to explore further the parallels between the cat's behavior and human character. For example, to extend the analogy further, you could talk about the fact that cats that get stuck in trees sometimes need to be rescued by people. Similarly, people sometimes need help to get themselves out of trouble.

Once you've chosen a parallel to examine, consider how the analogy can help students better understand and improve a situation or habit. For example, the person who's in a dangerous situation could turn to a trusted adult for help—analogous to the person who rescues the cat from the tree.

While analogies can be very effective, it's helpful to be aware of a few potential pitfalls that you may encounter when teaching with analogical stories. Keep the following ideas in mind as you use this book.

Emphasize the key concept. Make sure your students remember the character content of what you're trying to teach with an analogy—not just the analogy. It would be easy to spend a lot of time discussing the fascinating box jellyfish (page 25), but ultimately get distracted by this conversation from the lesson's larger ideas, such as not judging people by their appearances. Be careful not to let the analogy's starting point draw all the attention to itself and overpower the character messages you're working to convey.

Share the necessary background information. Students must understand the first symbol or object before making an analogy to the target concept. For example, perhaps you want to discuss the positive behavior of making wise decisions, and you decide to use the lesson on the Venus flytrap (page 145). This story provides basic background information so that your students will understand some of the relevant qualities of the Venus flytrap. If your group still has questions, be sure to try to answer these before moving on with your analogy. Then, once all of you understand and grasp the starting point of the analogy, you can begin exploring the parallels to human character and to avoiding risky behaviors.

Clarify distinctions. Make sure your students understand how the two objects of an analogy *differ* to avoid confusion or misconceptions. You might compare a thunderstorm to a temper tantrum. But this does not mean that a thunderstorm is an angry cloud. It's a phenomenon of nature. And although LuLu the pig (page 122) acted quickly to save her owner's life, it does not mean that pigs have the same cognitive abilities or emotional capacity as humans.

Limit anthropomorphizing. Remember that it can be easy for kids to blur the lines between reality and imagination. Many plants and animals have human-like characteristics. But be sure that students understand that a bristlecone pine tree (page 29), for example, doesn't truly have traits such as patience or strength of character in the same way that a person would.

Don't allow name-calling. It would be wrong to label a person as a cuttlefish (page 51) simply because he or she exhibits some traits that are analogous to those of the cuttlefish. Whether you say that someone is a bragger or that someone is a cuttlefish, you're using a label. Make name-calling forbidden in your classroom.

Check the facts. Make sure that your facts are accurate when making analogies, and avoid making invalid analogies or extensions to your analogy. Almost anything, under the right conditions, can be generally said to be "like" something else, so beware of taking an analogy to a false or incomplete conclusion. Be mindful of where comparisons break down, and be careful not to create misunderstanding by assuming that the familiar object and the target are the same in all ways. Make sure that your students understand the differences between them.

How to Use This Book

Analogies can be very powerful for teaching many subjects, including character education. Are you eager to tap into that power? This book gives you a wide range of quick and simple ways to do so. You'll get your students actively thinking about character, while also engaging their interest in nature.

You may want to begin by helping kids get the hang of analogies. Pass out copies of the Getting Started with Analogies worksheet (on the CD-ROM) and invite students to fill in their answers. Do an example together, if that's helpful. Then, once everyone has completed the sheet, talk about how kids answered. Discuss different interpretations. If appropriate, explain why some analogies are logical and others are not.

When kids are familiar with analogies, you can jump into one of this book's twenty-five lessons. Each one is centered on a story that explores the characteristics and qualities of a fascinating plant, animal, or other object from nature. You don't have to use these lessons or stories in any order. You can choose one that relates to something else your class is studying, one that addresses a character trait you want to address, or simply one that sounds especially interesting. If you want to discuss or explore a certain character trait with your students, you can also refer to the Character Key Word Reference Chart on page 13. It offers a quick overview of which lessons explore specific traits.

When you've chosen a lesson, read the story to familiarize yourself with it before using it in class. Unlike the rest of the book, the stories are written directly to students, in kid-friendly language. However, if you think that some of the character vocabulary may be challenging for your students, check the Character Key Word Glossary on page 156 for kid-friendly definitions. Once you're ready to present a lesson to your group, you may choose to pass out copies of the story handout to students. You can then read the story aloud as kids follow along, invite volunteers to read passages, have kids read to themselves, or place kids in small groups to read the story together, making yourself available to answer questions or help with vocabulary. If you like, you can display the picture of the lesson's subject on an interactive whiteboard or other surface. (All pictures are on the included CD-ROM.)

Accompanying each story is a list of discussion questions that make connections between the story and character. These questions will help you lead your students to drawing analogies between the animals and plants explored in the lesson and human character traits and behaviors. Keep in mind that these questions are simply jumping-off points. Feel free to create your own analogies! By drawing upon your own experiences—and those of your students—you can find many more ways to think about and explore the lesson.

Similarly, the sample answers following each question are just to get you started. Be open to letting your group's conversation take its own course. Your students may surprise you with the intuitive comments and analogous connections they make on their own.

Along with the discussion questions, you'll find a short sidebar with additional fascinating facts about the lesson's animal or plant. You can use these facts to spark kids' interest and inspire additional research or exploration.

Each story is also accompanied by several activities that are specifically related to the lesson's character key words and to its animal or plant. These activities will help you engage your students in a deeper exploration of character and nature. Most require only minimal preparation and basic materials, and many include prepared handouts, which you will also find on the CD-ROM. These activities can be adapted to work with kids of different ages, interests, abilities, and needs. You know your group best. Do what works for you.

If you want to take a lesson even further, turn to pages 9–12. There you'll find descriptions of more than twenty activities that can be used in connection with any of the book's stories.

And before you dive in, a quick note about what this book *is* and what it *is not*:

Building Character with True Stories from Nature is *not* a book that defines in a scholarly way the many different methods for facilitating character education. But you *will* find the elements of good character education instruction throughout the book. You will find service learning components, based on authentic need and using student voice. You will find elements of cooperative learning, discussions of moral dilemmas, and ideas for thoughtful reflection. The book's activities incorporate student problem-solving and class meetings. And throughout, you will find natural and useful connections to your curriculum.

Each lesson focuses on specific character traits such as integrity, respect, and responsibility. Rather than presenting these ideas in a didactic way—which is unlikely to make a positive lasting impact on your students—you can use the book's lessons to explore character through analogies, while also supporting discovery, problem-solving, and other high-level thinking skills that are integral to learning and to good teaching. Most importantly, *Building Character with True Stories from Nature* presents another strategy for developing good character traits—that of using analogies from nature. These analogies—by engaging the brain and the emotions—can have a powerful effect on your students, leading to positive behavior habits and a deeper understanding of character.

The brain is adaptable, flexible, and capable of amazing development—especially in kids. This means that your students can choose to build and strengthen positive character traits such as patience, responsibility, and integrity. They can also work to overcome and change negative habits. And you can help them do this. Through the use of powerful analogies between nature and character, you can guide your students in creating and practicing character habits that are positive for themselves and for others.

I would love to hear how *Building Character with True Stories from Nature* works for you and your students. Please feel free to share your experiences by emailing me at help4kids@freespirit.com, or by writing to me in care of the following address:

Free Spirit Publishing
217 Fifth Avenue North, Suite 200
Minneapolis, MN 55401-1299

Best wishes to you,

Barbara A. Lewis

Character-Building Activities

You can use these activities with any of the lessons or stories in this book. These activities will help develop your students' analogical reasoning, build and strengthen positive character habits, and encourage productive discussion and reflection.

Quick Picks

Whether you're looking for something simple and fun to fill a short period of time in your day or you want a quick warm-up activity to get your students ready for deeper thinking, use the suggestions below with your group.

- Take kids outside and ask them to look at the clouds above. What animals and plants do they see in the clouds? Seeing something within something else is a beginning step in analogical thinking. Ask kids to draw the outlines of clouds and, within these outlines, to draw what they see in the clouds. If you can't go outside, you can do this activity by displaying photographs of clouds on a projector or interactive whiteboard.

- Pair up students and ask them to sit facing their partners, without talking. When everyone is still and quiet, invite kids to try to figure out how their partners are feeling, just by looking closely at their faces, posture, and so forth. Learning to be a careful and thoughtful observer is one step in learning to draw strong analogies.

Concentrate on Character

When you want to focus closely on character, these activities provide a variety of ways to stimulate kids to think and talk about character traits and habits.

- As a group, choose an animal or plant to talk about. Brainstorm a list of the animal or plant's characteristics. Then talk about comparisons to human character traits. *Example:* A lion acts brave when it defends its den or its family. A boy is brave when he overcomes his stage fright and reads aloud in front of the class.

- Work backward. Choose a character trait to explore, such as cooperation, creativity, curiosity, or loyalty. Then talk with your group about analogies they can draw between this trait and things in the natural world, such as animals, plants, or weather phenomena. For example, if you decide to focus on cooperation, you could discuss the fact that many quaking aspen trees are connected underground. Their strength comes from their connectedness. Working with others can make people stronger, too.

- Choose one story from the book and examine the positive characteristics of the lesson's subject. Talk with your group about how everyone can practice developing or strengthening one of those characteristics for one week. For example, dogs appear to show forgiveness and caring for humans. Can kids practice forgiveness and empathy each day? Brainstorm specific ideas for doing so. At the end of the week, talk about the experience. Did kids find that practicing the trait or behavior got easier as the week went on? Invite kids to journal about their experiences and what they learn.

- Invite students to make lists of their favorite objects in nature. Then have each student pick five of the items on his or her list and brainstorm character analogies to these plants and animals. *Example:* A mouse is small and can seem timid. It hides in small, dark places. Mice hide to protect themselves. Do people sometimes stay isolated or closed off because they are afraid to reveal themselves? Can it be scary to leave somewhere familiar and venture into the unknown?

- Once formed, habits are strong, but they can take effort to develop. Try this activity with your group to work on positive habit forming.

  1. Think of a desired habit, such as getting homework done on time.

  2. Compare this habit with something in nature that demonstrates the trait. For example, turning in assignments on time can be compared to a horse's dependability (page 93).

  3. Think of a way to develop the positive behavior pattern. What steps would you take to learn to be dependable as a horse? What dependable qualities does a horse have that can be emulated?

  4. Think of ways to repeat the practice until it becomes a new habit of being dependable.

- Pass out handouts of one story to kids and ask them to highlight passages or facts that especially grab their attention. Use these as starting points for drawing analogies with character traits or human behaviors.

- Use a lesson's picture (on the CD-ROM) to spark ideas about character analogies. Hand out copies of the picture or display it on an interactive whiteboard or other screen. Ask kids to label different parts of the creature or plant and draw analogies between these parts and human character traits. For example, the trunk of an elephant could be labeled "reaching out to others in friendship."

- Ask students to write about personal experiences in which they demonstrated particular character traits. Then talk about drawing analogies between their situations and the traits of plants and animals in the book.

Play and Create

Getting kids active, engaged in language arts, and using their creative thinking skills will help reinforce messages and deepen understanding of character.

- Divide your group into pairs and tell kids that each pair will write and perform a skit. Assign two plants or animals to each pair and ask kids to act out a scene between these two "characters." For example, suppose one pair is assigned "dog" and "cat." What kind of scene could these animals share? Would they agree or disagree? How are they the same or different? Give kids time to work on their ideas and prepare their skits, and help as necessary. As time allows, have kids perform their skits for the group. If desired, you could spread out these performances over several days or even weeks. After each performance, discuss the ideas and analogies raised.

- Play the analogy game with your students. This works especially well after you have read all or most of the stories in this book, but you can apply it to a smaller group of lessons as well.

  Obtain a foam ball or other soft, squishy ball. One student begins as the leader and stands in front of the group, holding the ball. The leader says the name of something from nature, such as "tree," "cow," or "thunderstorm." Each group member quickly thinks of a quality (positive or negative) shown by the named object from nature. When students have their ideas in mind, they raise their hands. Then the leader calls on the first person whose hand he or she sees in the air, and throws the ball to that person. That person answers by saying the positive or negative quality, and then says the name of another object in nature and throws the ball to a third person whose hand is raised.

  Example: Jessie says "dolphin" and throws the ball to Lukas, who has his hand up. Lukas says "friendship." Then he says, "metalmark moth" and throws the ball to Senji, who is waving his arm. Senji catches the ball and says "copying." Play continues until everyone has had at least one turn.

  Variation: Divide your group into two teams. Have each team stand in a line, facing the opposite team. Throw the ball from person to person on opposite sides down the line, asking questions and giving answers. Establish a time limit for responses—possibly ten to fifteen seconds to ask or answer.

- Ask each kid to draw any plant or creature that he or she likes. Each day or so, invite a few students to show their drawings to the class. As a group, talk about what positive qualities the subject of each drawing might show. As the class brainstorms, write their answers and ideas on the board. Then choose one trait that is especially interesting and invite the group to write poems or short stories about this good quality and the animal or plant that shows it.

They could work individually or in small groups. Once they've finished, pair the artwork with the written work and create a display. As more kids present their artwork, the character display will continue to grow.

- Choose one of the animals or plants in the book and have kids write an acrostic poem using the first letters of the animal or plant's name, focusing on character traits and positive behaviors. Kids could do this individually and then share their compositions, or the group might brainstorm the poem together. For example:

  Dedicated
  Outgoing
  Good friend

- Invite kids to write fictional stories about an animal or plant from this book. Ask them to use their stories' plots to demonstrate connections between their animal or plant subjects and human character traits.

- Many people remember new information better when it's accompanied by music. Have your group compose and learn a song about an animal or plant and its characteristics. Challenge them to include as many details from the lesson as possible.

Beyond the Basics

These activities explore a range of subject areas and experiences, from science to service learning.

- **Science:** Using diagrams or models, investigate the internal structure of two plants or two animals. Compare and contrast them with your group. How are they similar? How are they different? Can you extend your findings into an analogy? *Example:* Bamboo and bristlecone pine cells have a somewhat similar structure even though the plants are very different. People, too, are often more alike than they appear on the surface.

- **Math:** Analogies are a big part of the study of math. Math analogies can be verbal, such as:

    Addition is to subtraction as multiplication is to division.

    Or math analogies can be numerical, such as:

    4 : 12 :: 1 : 3 or ¼ : 0.25 :: ½ : 0.5

    Use the structure of math analogies to talk with kids about character. For example, you might say, "Addition is to subtraction as helping each other is to _____ (hurting others)." Or, "Some types of bamboo (page 21) grow very quickly. What happens when a number is multiplied by itself? The number grows quickly, too. Are there habits you have that seem to grow quickly? When is this helpful? When can it be harmful?"

- **Social studies and history:** Write analogies from nature to famous people from history, or to local government or community leaders. Be sure to be respectful but insightful, and focus primarily on the positive character traits this person embodies. *Example:* Martin Luther King Jr. stood up for his beliefs and his values.

He stood strong like a bristlecone pine tree. He persevered in the difficult struggle for equal rights.

- **Service learning:** Service and character education go hand in hand. Plan and carry out a group learning project that gets kids involved in service. For example, read the stories about pigs (page 122), dolphins (page 69), elephants (page 81), or dogs (page 63). All of these stories describe animals that seem to show caring for something or someone else. Then brainstorm with your group about a local cause, organization, or need that kids care about. Ideas could include a community food shelf, homeless shelter, animal rescue organization, or library fundraiser. Vote on a project and create a plan, from volunteering at the food shelf to donating books to a library sale.

    After you've completed your project, talk with kids about the experience. What did they learn? How did doing service make them feel?

Character Key Word Reference Chart

Looking for a specific idea to investigate and discuss with your group?
Use this chart to find out which character traits are discussed in each lesson.

Character Key Word	Lesson #
Adaptability	8, 12, 18, 21, 24
Assertiveness	7
Balance	12, 26*
Caring	1, 5, 10, 11, 13, 25, 26*
Citizenship	9, 23, 26*
Communication	1, 5, 7, 18
Conservation	4, 11, 22, 26*
Cooperation	11, 12, 15, 19, 21, 25
Courage	6, 10, 16, 20
Curiosity	5, 22
Fairness and Equality	16, 23
Forgiveness	1, 10
Friendship	10, 13
Good Decision-Making	14, 16, 24, 26*
Hard Work	4, 9, 22
Helpfulness	1, 11
Honesty	6, 8, 14, 17

Character Key Word	Lesson #
Inner Strength	2, 4, 21
Integrity	8, 14, 16, 17, 21
Loyalty	10, 15, 19, 25
Patience	4
Peacefulness	13
Perseverance	4, 6, 15
Planning and Preparation	12, 22
Playfulness	5, 18
Problem Solving	2, 6, 7, 9, 11, 20
Respect	7, 11, 13, 17, 20, 23
Responsibility	2, 10, 15, 19, 23
Safety	3, 5, 17
Self-Control	3, 21, 24
Service	10, 15, 25
Tolerance and Acceptance	3, 7, 8, 9, 12, 13, 20, 23
Trust; Trustworthiness	1, 25
Wisdom and Learning	5, 18, 20

* Lesson 26 is a bonus lesson, which you can find on the CD-ROM.

Lesson 1
Apes

Character Key Words
Caring • Helpfulness • Communication • Trust • Forgiveness

Students will
- learn about apes, a group of mammals that includes gorillas and chimpanzees
- think about examples of helpfulness and caring, and apply these ideas to their own lives
- discuss and consider what might happen when someone treats an animal or a person with cruelty or with kindness
- compare the behavior of the chimpanzee Billy Jo with people who are willing to trust and forgive others, even after they have been hurt

Overview

Apes are among the most intelligent animals on the planet. They share close genetic ties with humans, and they demonstrate behaviors that seem similar to character traits in people. These traits include helpfulness, caring for others, and communication.

After learning the stories of gorillas named Binti Jua and Koko, and a chimpanzee named Billy Jo, students will enjoy discussing and considering what might happen if people treat animals, and other people, with kindness, love, and respect rather than anger and violence.

Story

Awesome Apes

Awesome Apes

It was a fun day at the Brookfield Zoo near Chicago. People crowded around the gorilla cage. They smiled as they watched the large apes play, nap, and eat.

But suddenly the day turned scary. A three-year-old boy fell into the cage.

A gorilla named Binti Jua saw what happened. With her own baby on her back, she hurried over to the toddler. Frightened zookeepers and tourists watched from above. Would she hurt him?

Binti Jua picked up the boy gently. She cuddled him. Then she protected him from the other gorillas. Her actions gave zookeepers time to enter the cage. They carried the little boy to safety.

Binti Jua helped the boy even though he wasn't a gorilla like her. She may have even saved his life.

Another famous gorilla is Koko. Her trainer, Francine, taught her hundreds of words in sign language. Scientists aren't sure just what Koko understands. She probably doesn't think about language the same way people do. But Koko does communicate. Francine says that Koko used sign language to ask for a pet kitten. Koko played with the kitten and cuddled with it.

Many apes seem to be good helpers. Have you ever heard this saying? *I'll scratch your back if you'll scratch mine.* It means, "I'll help you if you'll help me." Apes seem to follow this saying. They help clean each other's fur. Sometimes they get food from each other in return.

From *Building Character with True Stories from Nature* by Barbara A. Lewis, copyright © 2012. Free Spirit Publishing Inc., Minneapolis, MN; 800-735-7323; www.freespirit.com. This page may be reproduced for use within an individual classroom. For all other uses, contact www.freespirit.com/company/permissions.cfm.

Chimpanzees are a kind of ape. Scientists have studied how chimps help each other. Sometimes they're helpful even when they don't get any reward. In some tests, they help people, not just other chimps.

Chimps and other apes also love to play. They wrestle and chase each other around. They laugh, too. Tickling and playing can give them the giggles.

So it seems like apes can be helpful and friendly. They can even be funny!

Apes also show fear—and trust. A chimpanzee named Billy Jo had good reasons to fear people. Humans had hurt Billy Jo badly. His first owners made him perform for audiences. Sometimes his owners hit him. Then, after fifteen years, they sold him. Billy Jo's new home was a medical lab. There, people did hundreds of medical experiments on him. He lived in a cage. He went through scary, painful tests.

Billy Jo grew terrified of people. When humans came toward his cage, he banged on the bars. Sometimes he bit his own hands in fear. Groups of people made him especially nervous.

But Billy Jo's story gets happier. He went to live at a special place for rescued chimps. Billy Jo was safe at last.

The people at Billy Jo's new home had to be patient with him. He was still scared. Sometimes he acted angry and wild. But with time and kindness, Billy Jo grew calmer. He was often sweet and gentle with people he trusted. Even after all he had been through, Billy Jo learned to open up to people again.

From *Building Character with True Stories from Nature* by Barbara A. Lewis, copyright © 2012. Free Spirit Publishing Inc., Minneapolis, MN; 800-735-7323; www.freespirit.com. This page may be reproduced for use within an individual classroom. For all other uses, contact www.freespirit.com/company/permissions.cfm.

Talk It Over

Use these questions to guide your students in considering analogies between apes and caring, forgiveness, helpfulness, and other character traits and behaviors in people.

Binti Jua took care of a little boy, even though he was very different from her. Can you think of ways that we can show caring toward people who seem to be different from us in some way?

- By learning more about people of different cultures, beliefs, and backgrounds. The more we learn about other people, the more we see how much we all have in common.

- By sharing stories with people about our backgrounds and our life experiences. Everyone has a different story, and we feel good when others listen to us and care about our stories.

- We might be able to help someone from another country learn to speak English.

- We could write letters to pen pals from other parts of the country or the world.

Ape Facts

In one study, chimps worked to help others get food, even though the helping chimps received no reward.

Orangutans are a type of ape. In the Malay language, *orangutan* means "person of the forest."

Gibbons are another type of ape. Using their long, flexible arms, they can swing through the jungle at up to 35 miles per hour.

Koko the gorilla communicates with people using sign language. Why do you think it's important for people to communicate with each other?

- When we talk with others about our thoughts and feelings—and listen to what they say, too—we get closer to other people. We build trust and understanding.

- Talking about things that make us feel worried or scared can make us feel better.

- When we are not open and honest, it can lead to misunderstandings and hurt feelings.

- It's important to communicate clearly so that everyone understands, especially when you have something important to say or share.

Scientists have seen chimpanzees perform caring acts for each other. What kind acts can you do for other people—friends, family, teachers, and others? (Encourage kids to brainstorm ideas for kind acts, large and small. Keep a list on the board or on mural paper, if you like.)

- If someone is new in class, we can be friendly and helpful. We can show the new student around, answer questions, and help the person feel comfortable in a new place.

- Everyone has different talents and skills. If you are good at math or reading, you could offer your help to someone who has a harder time with those subjects.

- Some kids don't have enough food or warm clothes. We can help get those things for them.

Doing something nice for someone else can often bring about kind actions from the person or animal that you help—but not always. Why and why not? Why might you want to be nice anyway?

- If someone has been nice to you, you want to be nice to them.

- We all have days when we're in a bad mood for one reason or another. At those times, it can make us feel better when people are nice to us. But other times we might be so cranky that we don't respond nicely. If you're kind to someone and they don't return your kindness right away, try again some other day.

- It makes you feel good inside to be nice to someone, even if they aren't nice back to you right away.

- Sometimes, if you keep being nice to someone who does or says mean things, that person may change his or her behavior. Giving kindness can bring out kindness in others. (If someone is mean to you again and again, talk to a grown-up you trust. Get help.)

Chimpanzees sometimes help each other even when they don't get any obvious reward. Do you think that people sometimes do nice things just to get a reward? Is that okay? What are some reasons other than a reward to do kind and helpful things?

- Even if someone does something nice in order to get a reward, the nice thing still gets done.

- Helping other people just makes you feel good inside. Doing the right thing is its own reward.

- Being kind and helpful to others can lead to other people being kind and helpful to us. It can also inspire people to be nice to others. Kindness spreads.

The chimpanzee Billy Jo learned to trust people again, even though people had hurt him in the past. How can *we* learn to trust people who have hurt us? Why is it sometimes important to do this? How do you tell the difference between people you can trust and those you probably should not trust?

- If someone who hurt you says he or she is sorry, and shows it with his or her actions, then it is easier to trust that person again.

- Everyone makes mistakes. We all deserve forgiveness and a second chance.

- Sometimes you need to be careful with your trust. It might be better—and safer—not to trust someone who has hurt you badly, or someone who makes you feel uncomfortable or unsafe.

Do you think that Billy Jo felt better when he learned to trust people again? Can people feel happier when they forgive and trust others? Why?

- Carrying around anger or hurt can make you feel really bad. Over time, it can even make you sick. Forgiving someone can make those bad feelings go away, even though it may take a while.

- If you don't trust other people, it's hard to make and keep friends. It can be a lonely feeling.

- When you trust someone, you're usually happy to be with that person. You feel safe. Trusting someone can also help you relax and be yourself.

Activities

Activity 1: Speaking with Signs

Materials
Sign Language Alphabet handout (on CD-ROM)

Directions
Help kids learn to sign the alphabet in American Sign Language. Pass out copies of the Sign Language Alphabet handout. As a group, choose a few short words to learn to spell. As students practice, talk about different ways of communicating. What would it be like if they *couldn't* communicate with others? How would that make them feel? Why is it important to be able to share our thoughts and emotions?

Activity 2: The Kindness Chorus

Materials
Optional: Colored pencils and/or pens

Directions
Divide the class into small groups of two to four. Have each group work together to write a song or rap about being kind to everyone, forgiving others, or helping others without rewards. Have kids write down their compositions, and hang their papers outside your room where other students can see and enjoy them.

Optional: Invite students to perform their songs or raps for another class or at a school assembly or other event.

Activity 3: Opposites Attract

Materials

2 bar magnets (or, if possible, several pairs of bar magnets)

Directions

In front of the class, hold up the two bar magnets and hold them with the two north poles close together. Show how the magnets push each other away. Next, do the same with the south poles. They will also repel each other. Invite kids to take turns holding the magnets so that they can feel how strongly the same magnetic poles repel each other.

Next, point the north pole of one bar magnet toward the south pole of the other magnet. They will pull together. Again, offer kids the chance to do this for themselves.

Variation: If you have enough magnets, divide the class into smaller groups and allow kids to experiment and play with the magnets as you lead the discussion.

Following this simple demonstration, lead your group in making analogies to friendships and other relationships. Like magnets, are people who are very different ever drawn to each other? Can they form strong friendships? Why do kids think that this is or isn't the case? What if two people are very similar? Can it sometimes be challenging for them to work together or to be friends? Why or why not?

Activity 4: Celebrate Diversity

Materials

Space to hold the event

Various music, food, family pictures, and other items to share and display

Volunteers to help oversee the event, if necessary

Directions

Hold a classroom celebration honoring and exploring diverse backgrounds and heritages. Invite families to bring favorite foods. Teach kids games from other parts of the world. Ask students to tell stories about their families or backgrounds, to perform songs they grew up singing, to display artwork that expresses their culture, or to take part in other activities celebrating diversity, individuality, and understanding.

Lesson 2
Bamboo

Character Key Words
Inner Strength • Problem Solving • Responsibility

Students will
- learn about bamboo's natural qualities, including its strength and its rapid growth
- draw analogies between bamboo's many uses and the ways people can think creatively to solve problems
- consider positive character traits such as inner strength and responsibility and talk about them with their peers
- discuss how small, negative behaviors can get quickly out of control

Overview
Kids will be fascinated by how fast bamboo grows, by its surprising strength, and by the many ways it can be used. Through discussion and activities, you can help your students see how these natural qualities are analogous to character traits and human behaviors including responsibility, strength, and problem solving. Help your students explore real-life situations that can quickly get out of control, just like bamboo's rapid growth. Your group may also enjoy talking about ways that people could creatively use bamboo and make the most of its natural characteristics to help people in need.

Story
Bountiful Bamboo

Bountiful Bamboo

Have you ever thought of building a house of grass? Bamboo is a type of grass. But it's very strong. People build homes from bamboo because they can even last through earthquakes and storms. These homes can stand for hundreds of years.

Bamboo grows in Asia, Africa, Australia, and North and South America. In other words, much of the world is home to some kind of bamboo.

Buildings are a good way to use bamboo. But this plant can do much more. Inventors have used tiny pieces of bamboo to do big jobs. Thomas Edison used thin strings of bamboo in his first lightbulbs. Alexander Graham Bell used a sharp sliver of bamboo as the needle in his first record player.

Bamboo is also a good air cleaner. It helps take unhealthy gases and chemicals out of the air. That makes air better for us to breathe.

Bamboo grows faster than almost any other plant. Some types of bamboo can grow more than 4 feet in a single day! Most trees take thirty to fifty years to grow from seeds to their full size. But some kinds of bamboo need just six months to grow up.

Fast-growing bamboo can cause trouble, too. Roots spread far and wide underground. Spiky young bamboo shoots pop up all over the place. They can even crack sidewalks or streets.

Have you ever eaten bamboo? Cooked bamboo shoots are tasty and tender. People in many countries eat it. Bamboo is also a giant panda's favorite food. Pandas eat up to 85 pounds of the plant each day. (They don't cook their bamboo, though.)

Could bamboo help feed people around the world? Because it grows so fast, it might be able to help a lot of hungry people.

Bamboo has so many surprising uses. What else could we do with bamboo?

From *Building Character with True Stories from Nature* by Barbara A. Lewis, copyright © 2012. Free Spirit Publishing Inc., Minneapolis, MN; 800-735-7323; www.freespirit.com. This page may be reproduced for use within an individual classroom. For all other uses, contact www.freespirit.com/company/permissions.cfm.

Talk It Over

Use these questions to guide your students in considering analogies between bamboo and inner strength, problem solving, and other character traits and behaviors in people.

The strength of bamboo might surprise you. Have you ever found strength in a surprising place?

- Someone unexpected stepped forward as a leader.

- In an emergency, you found inner strength and courage that you didn't know you had.

Bamboo is a sturdy, reliable material for building homes. What are strong, reliable "building materials" that you can use to build your life? How can you work on having more of these materials in your life?

- Dedicated work, good family and friends, education, and service to others can all be good "building materials" in your life.

- You can build a healthy life on a foundation of positive character traits such as honesty, responsibility, caring, fairness, forgiveness, cooperation, and good citizenship.

Tiny pieces of bamboo have been used to make important inventions, from Thomas Edison's lightbulb to Alexander Graham Bell's record player. What does this tell you?

- Every part of the whole is important, and even the smallest pieces have a function. Therefore, each small job is important for the proper functioning of the government, business, organization, school, team, and family.

- Every small part of the body has a purpose. Treat your body with care.

Some kinds of bamboo grow very, very quickly. What else can grow quickly or spread out of control quickly? (Encourage kids to consider, among other ideas, the way that a small mistake can sometimes lead to larger, more harmful mistakes.)

- Skipping homework or chores can quickly leave you far behind, making it hard to catch up.

- Rumors can spread quickly. They can cause hurt feelings and misunderstandings.

- Caring acts and friendly words can be contagious. So can laughter and smiles.

- Try to face smaller disagreements and talk them out before they destroy relationships.

- Take care of small health problems before they grow into more serious issues.

- Debt can grow rapidly when we don't save and spend wisely. Before you know it, you might have no money to spend. Try to save up your money before you buy, so that you know you can afford the purchase.

You might not think of using bamboo to build your house. But bamboo is a common building material in many countries. People use bamboo in many other creative ways, too. How can you connect this idea to problem solving?

- Sometimes thinking about things in new ways can help you solve tough problems.

- Creative thinking is a powerful tool for answering difficult questions.

- Many people have hidden talents.

Bamboo's fast growth could be very useful to people. With careful planting, we can continue to have lots of bamboo. This could be important, especially if people are using bamboo for food and for building homes. How could this connect to human behavior?

- Sometimes the ideas that come to your head the fastest are the ideas that you should look at most carefully.

- Building good character muscles can help you do better in all areas of your life—in school, family relationships and friendships, your homework, jobs, and so on.

- Once you start practicing, good character traits can grow quickly. They will help you make good decisions.

Bamboo Facts

Bamboo has a higher tensile strength than many alloys of steel and a higher compressive strength than many mixtures of concrete. It has a better strength-to-weight ratio than graphite.

In China, bamboo has long been used to treat infections.

Flutes made from bamboo are traditional instruments in many Asian countries.

Activities

Activity 1: Character of Bamboo

Materials

Small slips of paper (2 per student)
2 containers for slips (hats, jars, plastic cups)

Directions

In addition to being a building material, a food, and a material for inventors, bamboo was once used as a writing surface. Many hundreds of years ago in China, people used thin slips of bamboo in place of paper.

Give each student two small slips of paper. Ask each student to write a character word on one slip. (*Examples: honesty, responsibility, integrity.*) On the second slip, ask each student to write a word describing bamboo. (*Examples: strong, tall, grass.*) Put the character slips into one container, and the bamboo slips into the other container. Ask a volunteer to draw one slip from each container and read the two words aloud. As a group, discuss whether there are analogies between the two ideas. If so, what are they? Why do these analogies work? If the group does not see a valid analogy, why not? Continue with additional slips as time allows.

Activity 2: Growth of Bamboo

Materials

1 unused compressed sponge
Bowl or jar
Water (with food coloring, if desired)

Directions

Bamboo's fast growth is sometimes helpful and sometimes harmful, depending on the situation. Demonstrate how a little bit of an outside factor or influence—whether positive or negative—can lead to big results.

Place the dry sponge in a bowl or jar and begin pouring a small amount of water on it to show how a relatively small amount of liquid—drip, drip, drip—can have a big effect. As the sponge grows and expands, talk with the group about analogous situations in human behavior and human character.

Activity 3: Bamboo Haiku

Materials

Optional: Bamboo Haiku handout (on CD-ROM)

Directions

In Japan, one of the many countries where bamboo thrives, haiku is a traditional form of poetry, which usually explores the natural world and also human emotion. Have each student write a haiku about bamboo, connecting it to a relevant character trait. For example:

Bamboo, reaching high (*5 syllables*)
Stretching to the skies above (*7 syllables*)
So strong—so silent (*5 syllables*)

For younger students, it may be helpful to use the Bamboo Haiku handout. Show kids how to fill in each space with one syllable.

After everyone has had time to write a poem, invite volunteers to share their poems with the group. You could also post poems on a bulletin board in class, or create a compilation for kids to take home and share with their families.

Activity 4: Watch It Grow

Materials

2 small bamboo plants (available at a local nursery or an online nursery)

Directions

Purchase both a fast-growing tropical bamboo plant and a small, slower growing pigmy bamboo plant. Care for them in your classroom or space, and monitor their growth over time. See how quickly the fast-growing one gets bigger. Compare this to rapidly spreading rumors. Talk with kids about preventing or stopping rumors, lies, and other harmful talk that can sometimes get out of control.

Lesson 3
Box Jellyfish

Character Key Words
Safety • Self-Control • Tolerance and Acceptance

Students will
- learn about the box jellyfish and its dangerous poison
- draw analogies between the box jellyfish's enticing appearance and activities that seem fun but may be dangerous
- discuss the consequences of actions and behaviors and consider how things are not always what they seem
- discuss the value of exercising self-control and think about how to stay safe in potentially dangerous situations

Overview
The box jellyfish lesson is one of the more serious ones in this book. It takes a close look at temptation, danger, and other weighty ideas. It also covers a fascinating creature. Kids will be intrigued by the box jellyfish's beauty and by its deadly poison. As students learn about the box jellyfish—which is tempting in appearance—they will draw analogies to human activities. Some experiences may seem fun and exciting, but can quickly put kids in dangerous and harmful situations. Students will understand that they are free to choose what they do, but they may not always know or choose exactly what the consequences might be. At the same time, kids will consider the pitfalls of judging people based on appearance.

Story
Box Jellyfish—Beautiful but Deadly

Box Jellyfish—Beautiful but Deadly

You might not even see it at first. The box jellyfish is pale blue and transparent. It's almost invisible. It moves through the water with a dancer's gentle grace.

But beware! This delicate beauty is a dangerous beast. Even its other names sound scary. *Marine stinger. Sea wasp.* These names come from the jellyfish's deadly sting.

Most jellyfish drift wherever the ocean takes them. But not box jellies. They move themselves through the water as they hunt. They eat shrimp, fish, and other sea creatures. They have twenty-four eyes to help them find food.

Box jellyfish live in waters around Australia, Hawaii, and the Caribbean Islands. These delicate jellies are silent and hard to spot, even though they have up to fifteen long tentacles. Each tentacle can be ten feet long. And each one has about 5,000 stinging cells.

Box jellyfish stings are very, very painful. Even worse, the stinging cells carry deadly poison.

If a swimmer gets stung, acting quickly is important. The person needs medicine within twenty or thirty minutes. Otherwise, he or she may die. Swimmers who have been stung have died from heart attacks and from drowning.

Of course, the best way to stay safe is not to get stung at all. Many divers wear suits that protect them. Others avoid beaches where jellies live.

But here's some good news. There is a quick and simple way to help someone who has gotten stung. Put vinegar on the sting. It stops more poison from getting into the body. So be prepared. If you swim where the jellies prowl, take some vinegar with you. It may save a life. But sorry—vinegar won't take away the pain. Only time can do that.

From *Building Character with True Stories from Nature* by Barbara A. Lewis, copyright © 2012. Free Spirit Publishing Inc., Minneapolis, MN; 800-735-7323; www.freespirit.com. This page may be reproduced for use within an individual classroom. For all other uses, contact www.freespirit.com/company/permissions.cfm.

Talk It Over

Use these questions to guide your students in considering analogies between box jellyfish and safety, self-control, and other behaviors and character traits in people.

The box jellyfish is beautiful, but very dangerous. What are some things that may be tempting to people but can also be dangerous or unhealthful?

- Disobeying your parent or teacher
- Eating too much junk food or not exercising enough
- Ignoring your beliefs or goals in order to be popular
- Hanging out in dangerous places that appear exciting
- Trying cigarettes, alcohol, or other harmful substances

The box jellyfish is not exactly what it appears to be. Can you think of ways to compare this to meeting new people or forming ideas about others?

- You might think that someone isn't very interesting or exciting when you first meet him or her. But often, when we get to know people better, we find out that we really like them.
- It's not a very good idea to judge people by the way they dress, the music they like, or the food they eat. It's what a person is like inside that is important.

The box jellyfish often swims near beaches that are popular with people. To stay safe from these jellies, swimmers need to be careful and prepared. In your life, what are some good ways that you can be safe?

- Always let a parent know where you are.
- Avoid talking with strangers.
- Be home before it gets dark outside.
- Try to walk with friends rather than alone.

- Make sure to have permission before looking at websites. If you ever see or read something online that makes you uncomfortable, confused, or scared, talk to a grown-up you trust.

A box jellyfish sting can kill a person within twenty to thirty minutes. What are some other things that can quickly become very dangerous?

- Sometimes a disagreement or a fight can get very serious and even scary in a short amount of time.
- A bad storm can get dangerous quickly. It's important to be aware of what's going on around you, and to know where to go to be safe.
- Sometimes people get addicted to drugs or alcohol even if they only try them once. It's important to think carefully about an activity's risks and dangers before making a decision.
- A situation that seems safe at first might not be. It's important to make careful choices about where you go and which people you spend time with.

It's very important to be aware and act quickly after being stung by a box jellyfish. Can you think of any other times when you might need to act quickly to keep yourself safe?

- Follow your good instincts. If you're in a situation where you feel uncomfortable or scared, find someone to help you.
- You need to be careful and aware when you're crossing streets.
- It's important to pay attention to your health. If you feel sick but ignore the signs, you might get sicker.

Using vinegar is a simple way to protect the body after a box jellyfish sting. What kind of protection do you have against harmful choices and dangerous situations?

- You can develop strong character muscles by thinking about, talking about, and practicing good character. These muscles will help you make positive choices.

- When you feel afraid or worried, talk to a grown-up you trust.

- Think before you act.

Box Jellyfish Facts

The box jellyfish's sting and venom do not affect sea turtles, which eat the jellies.

A group of jellyfish is called a smack.

A box jellyfish can weigh more than 4 pounds.

Activities

Activity 1: Vinegar Words

Materials

Vinegar Words handout (on CD-ROM)
Colored pencils (2 per student)

Directions

Pass out copies of the Vinegar Words handout and give each student two pencils of different colors. In the column marked Jellyfish Words, ask kids to use one color to write down some harmful character traits, behaviors, and ideas related to the box jellyfish. These descriptions might include: *not what it seems to be, tempting,* or *dangerous.* Then ask them to use the other pencils to write down Vinegar Words in the other column—positive character words and ideas that can counteract the harmful ones. For example:

Jellyfish Words — Vinegar Words
Tempting — Self-control

When kids have filled in the handouts, invite them to share some of their ideas. Talk about these as a group and discuss how positive character habits can act as vinegar against negative ones.

Activity 2: What If?

Materials

None

Directions

Sit in a circle. Describe a situation in which kids would need to make good choices. Emphasize safety and self-control. Then go around the circle, giving each student a chance to describe a positive way to handle the situation.

For example, you could ask the group, **What if you were home alone and a stranger called to ask for your parent? What would you do?** Possible responses could include, "I would hang up and call a neighbor or friend," or, "I would say, 'She can't talk right now' or 'He's busy.'"

Or you could ask students, **What would you say if a friend offered you a cigarette?** Kids might answer, "No, thanks," or "Nah. I think smoking smells gross."

Acknowledge and discuss that making these choices is not always easy.

Activity 3: Jellyfish Jargon

Materials

Crayons, colored pencils, and/or markers

Directions

Invite kids to draw pictures of the box jellyfish, but instead of using regular lines to make the shape of the jellyfish, have them "draw" with words related to the jellyfish and its characteristics. For example, each of the jellyfish's tentacles could be a sentence or phrase, such as "Beautiful but deadly" or "Don't judge someone based on appearances." (*Note:* If needed, draw an example on the board to show kids how this idea works. Additionally, younger kids could draw basic pictures of jellyfish and then write words inside their drawings.)

Invite students to share their work. Talk about why they chose the words they did.

Lesson 4
Bristlecone Pine Trees

Character Key Words
Hard Work • Patience • Inner Strength • Perseverance • Conservation

Students will
- learn about the bristlecone pine's natural qualities, especially its ability to live hundreds or even thousands of years
- discuss how patience, perseverance, and hard work can bring good results and big rewards
- think about the importance of respecting and protecting our planet

Overview
The long lifespan of many bristlecone pine trees will amaze kids. The trees' fascinating longevity is an excellent starting point for conversations about patience and perseverance. The bristlecone pine's strength and resilience will also inspire discussions about dedication and hard work. The story of the bristlecone pine's difficult existence can lead students to understand that struggles and problems can sometimes help people grow stronger. And the trees' place in history offers a jumping-off point for talking about the value of environmental conservation and about the importance of respecting older people.

Story
Tough Bristlecone Pine Trees

Tough Bristlecone Pine Trees

What do you think the oldest living thing on Earth is?

A sea turtle?

An elephant?

That fuzzy stuff at the back of your fridge?

Nope. One of the oldest known living things on earth is the bristlecone pine tree. There are several kinds of bristlecone pines. They grow in Colorado, New Mexico, Arizona, Utah, Nevada, and California.

One of the oldest bristlecone pines is called Methuselah. Scientists think it is between 4,600 and 4,850 years old. It stands in eastern California's White Mountains. Don't go looking for it, though. Its exact spot is a secret to almost everybody. This is to keep the ancient tree safe.

Methuselah has been around for almost 5,000 years. That's a very long time. It can be a little hard to even imagine that many years. Think about it. That means:

Methuselah was a young tree when the pyramids were built in ancient Egypt.

It was already over 4,500 years old when the United States became a country.

It was around way, way, *way* before your great-great-grandfather was born.

The bristlecone pine tree lives in harsh places. Many of the trees are on high mountain slopes. Strong winds sweep past them. Icicles droop from their branches. Very little rain falls for their thirsty roots and needles to soak up.

From *Building Character with True Stories from Nature* by Barbara A. Lewis, copyright © 2012. Free Spirit Publishing Inc., Minneapolis, MN; 800-735-7323; www.freespirit.com. This page may be reproduced for use within an individual classroom. For all other uses, contact www.freespirit.com/company/permissions.cfm.

Yet the pines thrive. Their branches twist and turn white. But they are strong.

Bristlecone pines are related to giant sequoia trees. Bristlecone pines are much smaller than their cousins. Sequoias tower dramatically. Being big isn't always better, though. The small, dense bristlecone pines are strong and have very long lives. Why?

One reason bristlecone pines live so long is that they grow very slowly. In some years, they barely grow at all. If too little rain falls one season, these trees almost go to sleep. Maybe this sounds a bit boring to you. But growing slowly makes the pines' wood dense and strong. The trees can resist bugs and other threats.

Bristlecone pines have another secret, too. They grow in places where very few plants can survive. That means that these trees don't have to share soil and water with many other plants.

Some bristlecone pines do grow lower on mountain slopes. They grow faster than the trees higher up. The weather is warmer. The wind doesn't bend down the trees' trunks. The soil is rich and wet. But these pines don't live to be nearly as old as the ones that struggle to survive on higher, harsher slopes. Methuselah's long life is the tree's reward for endurance and hard work. And the view is great from up there, too!

From *Building Character with True Stories from Nature* by Barbara A. Lewis, copyright © 2012. Free Spirit Publishing Inc., Minneapolis, MN; 800-735-7323; www.freespirit.com. This page may be reproduced for use within an individual classroom. For all other uses, contact www.freespirit.com/company/permissions.cfm.

Talk It Over

Use these questions to guide your students in considering analogies between bristlecone pine trees and patience, perseverance, and other character traits and behaviors in people.

Bristlecone pine trees grow very slowly, which makes their wood very strong. How does this idea relate to people and the work they do? You might also ask, **Is it hard to be patient sometimes? Why? What are some values of patience?**

- If you take the time to do a job right, you'll probably make something better in the end.

- The faster way to do something isn't always the best way.

- Relationships take time to grow. The time that we spend with a person—facing challenges together, sharing experiences, and learning more about each other—builds a stronger and more lasting relationship.

Bristlecone pines that grow at lower altitudes don't live so long as the ones growing in harsher places. Can you think of ways to compare this idea to people's experiences?

- Challenges can build strong character. By working through problems, you can develop other strengths, such as patience, endurance, understanding, sympathy, caring, and so on.

- The easier path can be very tempting, but it's not always the most rewarding or productive.

- A big accomplishment is often the result of a lot of struggle and hard work.

Some bristlecone pines that are alive now were around for a lot of big events in the past. Why is this important? How does the long life of bristlecone pines relate to people's lives?

- If we cut down or harmed these old trees, we'd be losing a piece of history.

- It's important to protect nature and make sure plants and animals are still around for future generations.

- Older people have seen and experienced many things during their lives. As people age, their hands may grow gnarled and faces become wrinkled. But a person's character can grow stronger and stronger, especially if he or she has been kind and helpful to others.

The bristlecone pine is related to the giant sequoia tree. Bristlecone pines are much smaller than the soaring sequoias, which are also called giant redwoods. But bristlecone pines can live much longer. Does being the biggest person mean that you are the best or the strongest? What kinds of character traits make a person strong?

- Inner strength of character can make a person strong so that he or she can work through problems and hardships. Qualities such as patience, hard work, and perseverance can help you grow stronger, regardless of your size.

- Being kind and friendly to other people is a type of strength. You don't have to be the biggest or strongest person physically to show strong character.

Bristlecone Pine Tree Facts

The tallest bristlecone pine is just 60 feet tall. The tallest known sequoia is almost 380 feet tall.

Often, ancient bristlecone pines are part living and part dead. The living part of the tree continues to grow, often on the side of the tree away from the wind.

In 1964, a bristlecone pine called Prometheus, which is estimated to have been close to 5,000 years old at the time, was cut down.

Activities

Activity 1: Methuselah Mobile

Materials

Printouts of bristlecone pine tree picture (on CD-ROM)

Hole punch

String or yarn

Cardstock or construction paper

Kid-safe scissors

Colored pencils, crayons, or markers

Twigs, sticks, or dowels (2 or 3 per student)

Directions

Hand out copies of the bristlecone pine picture. Invite students to cut their bristlecone pine pictures into a few pieces, however they like. Punch a hole at the top of each picture piece. If desired, kids can add color or designs to the pictures. Next, have students each cut out a few pieces of cardstock or construction paper in any shapes they like, and have them write a character word describing bristlecone pine trees on each cutout. (*Examples: strong, sturdy, dependable, patient, enduring.*) Punch a hole in each character cutout.

Assemble mobiles. Help kids use yarn or string to connect the twigs or dowels, and to hang the tree pictures and character cutouts from these supports. Finally, attach a string to the top of the mobile so kids can hang them up in the classroom or at home.

As kids work, guide them in a discussion about the bristlecone pine's characteristics and their analogies to human qualities. How can these trees inspire us to build our character muscles? Do the trees display any traits that we would *not* want to have?

Variation: If possible, take a short nature walk with students to gather the twigs for their mobiles. Remind kids only to pick up twigs and sticks that have already fallen. As you walk, talk about respecting and protecting nature.

Activity 2: Map It Out

Materials

Map It Out handout (on CD-ROM)

Where Do Bristlecone Pines Grow? handout (on CD-ROM)

Colored pencils or crayons

Directions

Pass out copies of the Map It Out handouts. Pass out the Where Do Bristlecone Pines Grow? handout as well, or project it on a board or screen. Have younger kids color in the states where bristlecone pines grow. Invite older kids to chart the tree's habitat more precisely. Discuss how the altitude where the trees grow affects their longevity. Compare this idea to people who live in harsh or difficult conditions. Can going through hard times ever make people stronger? How and why? What other rewards does perseverance bring?

Activity 3: Tree-Ring Timelines

Materials

Tree-Ring Timeline handout (on CD-ROM)

Pencils, markers, pens

Optional: Thumbtacks, yarn, and paper

Directions

Pass out copies of the Tree-Ring Timeline handout. Explain to kids how the rings inside a tree's trunk show us how much the tree grew and when. The very smallest inside rings represent the tree's earliest years, while the outside rings come from the tree's most recent growth.

Ask kids to mark their birth dates on the handout, reminding them that their birth years will be near the outside of the tree, since this cross-section is from a very old bristlecone pine tree.

Then have kids mark other dates in their lives, as well as events in world history. Encourage students to think broadly about different countries and cultures, as well as about different kinds of history—not just political events, but also milestones in art, literature, sports, and more. Help them look up accurate information online or in print resources. As kids work, you could lead a discussion about perseverance and patience. What are challenges that kids face? How do they persevere through tough times? How can patience help us face problems? And how can overcoming problems make us stronger?

Lesson 5
Cats

Character Key Words
Curiosity • Playfulness • Safety • Wisdom and Learning • Communication • Caring

Students will
- compare cats' curiosity, intelligence, playfulness, and ways of communicating to human behaviors
- explore the value and the potential drawbacks of curiosity as well as its benefits
- think and talk about the ways we don't always have control of the consequences that follow choices we make

Overview
Cats are famous for their curiosity. Sometimes cats find themselves in dangerous places because of that. A cat that gets stuck high up in a tree is similar to a person who doesn't think through potential problems or risks before acting.

But cats are also underestimated for their intelligence. Cats learn by observing and imitating, and through trial and error. Cats have also rescued humans and animals from danger. And cats communicate their moods through use of their ears, fur, whiskers, eyes, and tails, and with sounds such as purring and hissing.

Story
Curious Cats

Curious Cats

Did curiosity *really* kill the cat?

Cats are natural adventurers. They like to explore new places. Sometimes their curiosity gets them into tight spots. A cat named Blackie lived in a New York City apartment. One day he decided to explore the apartment's chimney. Cats are good at climbing up. But their claws curl the wrong way to head back down. Blackie got stuck. Halfway up the chimney, he couldn't get down. He meowed for help. Finally a person had to rescue him. Blackie was badly hurt.

Cats can't always rescue themselves. They have helped others, though. You might think cats and dogs are enemies. And it's true that they don't always get along. But a cat in Rhode Island saved the family's dog. The dog was outside, and it was getting dark. Suddenly, the cat started jumping at the door. She did it over and over.

The owner was curious. What was making his cat act so strangely? He went outside to find out. There the owner saw a coyote. The little black dog was in its jaws. Yikes! The man shooed away the coyote. It dropped the dog and took off. The dog was scared, but safe—thanks to her pal, the cat. Somehow, the cat seemed to know that the dog was in trouble.

Cats have also rescued people. Cats have warned their owners about fires and dangerous gas leaks. They've saved them from snakes and from animal attacks. Police even think a cat in Columbus, Ohio, speed-dialed 911 when his owner needed help.

You may have noticed that many dogs are trained to sit, roll over, and fetch. Cats are less likely to do what you tell them. Does

From *Building Character with True Stories from Nature* by Barbara A. Lewis, copyright © 2012. Free Spirit Publishing Inc., Minneapolis, MN; 800-735-7323; www.freespirit.com. This page may be reproduced for use within an individual classroom. For all other uses, contact www.freespirit.com/company/permissions.cfm.

that mean that dogs are smarter? It's hard to compare. Different animals have different kinds of intelligence. But scientists know one thing for sure. Cats are no dummies. They have very good memories. They can learn by watching other cats or by watching people.

You can learn from watching your cat, too. If you look closely, you'll see that cats tell you how they feel. When your cat rubs against you, he is claiming you as his own. (You might think your cat belongs to *you*, but he probably has other ideas.) If he rolls over and shows his tummy, it means he really trusts you. If he swishes his tail quickly, presses back his ears, or hisses, be careful. That means he is angry, annoyed, upset, or afraid. But when his tail waves back and forth slowly, he is calm and happy.

Cats make wonderful pets and devoted friends. They can be loving and warm. And they're very playful. Cats love to pounce on toy mice, play with string, or chase flashlight beams. But cats are also very independent, and they can be pretty stubborn. So if you call your cat's name, she probably won't come running. She may be exploring a hole in the wall, or water dripping from a drainpipe. Or she might just be taking a catnap.

From *Building Character with True Stories from Nature* by Barbara A. Lewis, copyright © 2012. Free Spirit Publishing Inc., Minneapolis, MN; 800-735-7323; www.freespirit.com. This page may be reproduced for use within an individual classroom. For all other uses, contact www.freespirit.com/company/permissions.cfm.

Talk It Over

Use these questions to guide your students in considering analogies between cats and curiosity, communication, and other character traits and behaviors in people.

Like cats, people are often curious. What are some positive ways of being curious? How is curiosity related to learning?

- Being curious about new ideas often leads to learning. Learning in school teaches you things that are interesting and useful.

- Learning new skills can be fun. And when you learn to do something new—like play basketball, ice skate, play the guitar, or paint pictures—you can share that skill or talent with others.

- You can use many new skills to help others. Learning how to be a good citizen lets you help your community. Skills such as first aid can be lifesaving. And if you learn positive character traits, you can help others build their character muscles, too.

Curious cats sometimes get into dangerous spots. What are some ways that people can also run into trouble because of their curiosity?

- You can put yourself in danger when you explore an unsafe place, such as an old building or a construction site, or by going exploring in any unfamiliar place, especially by yourself.

- Kids can get in trouble when they go someplace with a stranger or open the door to a stranger.

- Exploring on the Internet without a grown-up can be dangerous.

- You may be really curious to see movies or play video games that are for older kids or for adults. But afterward, you might feel confused or scared.

Cats can't know or control what will happen as a result of their curiosity or exploring. People are free to choose what they do but can't always control the consequences that follow. What kinds of things do people do that can have negative results?

- Sometimes kids don't do their homework. Then they may fall behind in class, or they might get poor grades.

- If someone ate too much junk food, he or she wouldn't be healthy.

- A kid might ice skate on thin ice and fall into the cold water.

- Someone might make friends with a stranger on the Internet and then get into a scary or confusing situation.

- A person might steal something and then be in very serious trouble.

- If a person lies a lot, other people will probably stop trusting him or her.

- If you don't wear warm clothes when it's cold, or if you don't wash your hands when they're dirty, you might get sick.

Cat Facts

Cats have excellent memories. Studies have shown that a cat's short-term memory lasts up to 10 minutes, compared to less than a minute in humans. Another study showed that cats could remember a piece of information for up to 16 hours.

Some breeds of domesticated cats can run 30 miles per hour.

A cat's taste buds cannot detect sweet flavors.

Cats can communicate in many ways: with their tails, ears, whiskers, and more. How do people communicate without words?

- People can communicate with their eyes, mouths, and more. Sometimes people's facial expressions don't match what they're saying with words.

- People communicate through their posture and gestures—the ways they hold and move their bodies.

- Some people are very good at imagining and understanding how other people feel and think, even without any words.

Cats are very playful. Is it good to play? Can playing ever lead to problems?

- Some kinds of playing can spark your creativity. But if you play so much that you ignore your homework, you might not learn the things you need to know.

- Playing is fun and can help you relax and feel happy. But if you only play, you can start to get bored.

- You can make good friends when you play. But it's also important to do your chores and help your family at home.

Cats might be smarter than people recognize. They learn and communicate. Do people sometimes have talents or knowledge that others ignore or don't notice at first? Why do you think people do this?

- Sometimes we ignore what other people can do because we don't want to feel like they are smarter or more talented than we are. But everyone has different gifts. We're all good at something—and no one is good at everything.

- Sometimes we might make assumptions about what other people can do based on how they dress, speak, or look. But these assumptions are not always right. If we don't look deeper, we might never find out what interesting things other people can really do.

- Everyone has wisdom to share. It's important to value and listen to what other people have to say.

Cats have helped people and animals. Can you think of ways that you can help care for someone who needs help?

- We can help people in need by donating clothes, food, blankets, and other items.

- If we notice that someone at school seems lonely, we could be friendly to them and ask them to play with us.

- We can help our environment by recycling, turning off lights, and riding bikes instead of riding in cars.

- We can help animals in need by volunteering at animal shelters.

- We can raise money for people who need help in our own communities or around the world.

- We can offer to help people in our own families with chores, homework, or other tasks.

Activities

Activity 1: Cat Tales

Materials
None

Directions
Divide your class into small groups of four or five students each. Explain that they'll be writing chain stories about cats. When you write a chain story, one person begins by writing down a sentence or two. Then that student passes the paper to the next person, who adds some action to the story with another sentence or two. Then he or she passes it to another person, and so on.

Have each group focus on a certain character trait related to cats. One group could focus on a curious cat, while another could make up a story about a cat that helps someone. Another could write about a playful kitten.

Give the groups time to write, making sure that every student gets the chance to write at least twice.

Then ask groups to read their stories to the class. As a big group, talk about the ideas that the stories address and any questions that they raise.

Activity 2: Cat Scenes

Materials
Cat Scenes handout (on CD-ROM)
Scissors
Hat or other container for charades prompts

Directions
Before class, print out the handout and cut out the individual prompts. Mix the prompt slips together in a hat, bowl, or other container.

Explain the game of charades to the class. Rather than splitting up into teams, have all kids guess as a group, making the goal simply to figure out the activity being pantomimed and to correctly identify what catlike character trait it represents.

Ask for volunteers to be the actors. Have each actor show you the prompt before he or she begins pantomiming. If kids get stuck, help guide them toward the answer.

Play as many rounds as you have time for. Afterward, talk as a group about how difficult it is to communicate without words, and whether nonverbal communication can ever be better than using words. Why is communication important? What kinds of problems can come up without good communication?

Activity 3: Caring for Cats

Materials
Kitty Care handout (on CD-ROM)
Colored pencils or markers
Optional:
Contact information of local animal shelter
Permission slips from parents or guardians (if
    visiting an animal shelter)
Digital camera
Computer and photo printer
Poster board

Directions
Cats seem to care for others, and we can also care for cats. Hold a brainstorming session with kids to generate a list of tips and ideas for taking care of a pet cat. Help students look up accurate information online or in print resources. You could also call a local shelter or vet and ask if they have any advice for new cat owners.

Pass out copies of the handout and have kids each fill it in with the tips they think are most important or most interesting. Encourage them to add drawings or other decorations to the list if they like. Alternatively, choose as a group the tips that you most want to include on your list. Then enter these suggestions into the form on the computer and print out the completed form. However you create your list, make copies and distribute them to cat lovers, pet owners, local vets or shelters, and others who may be interested.

Variation: Take a class trip to visit a local no-kill animal shelter that has cats in need of homes. Take a camera with you, and take pictures of each cat (or several of them, if there are too many). Back at school, print out the photos and help kids use them to make a poster (or posters) inviting people to adopt homeless cats. Encourage kids to include cats' names and other information, if you have it, under the photos. (*Examples:* "Adopt Fluffy!" "Mittens loves tuna fish.") Put the shelter's contact information at the bottom. Hang up copies of your posters at school, and ask for permission to post them at the library, community center, and other locations as well.

Lesson 6
Coconut Crabs

Character Key Words

Honesty • Problem Solving • Perseverance • Courage

Students will

- learn some interesting information about coconut crabs, including their strong claws, and their shyness during the daytime, and compare their characteristics to human character traits

- consider the coconut crab's perseverance in working to crack open tough coconuts, and think about perseverance in people

- draw an analogy between the coconut crab's preference for nighttime and darkness and people who try to hide their actions from others

- compare the crab's daring behavior in entering people's homes to the courage that people can show in frightening situations

Overview

The coconut crab is a mysterious creature. It prefers the darkness of night to the bright daylight. It also seems to have a fondness for shiny objects, sometimes taking a chance and entering people's homes to take these treasures. But when the sun comes out, the crab disappears. Kids will find it interesting to compare this behavior to that of people who might lie or hide their actions to avoid blame or responsibility.

Besides coconuts, fruits, and seeds, the crab will devour injured animals and even wounded people. These 3- to 4-foot-long crabs live in the dense jungles of the Indo-Pacific islands. With their large size and fierce-looking claws, coconut crabs could be cast as monsters in a horror film. But coconut crabs are also problem solvers, and they work patiently and persistently to crack open coconuts for their sweet fruit.

Story

Creeping Coconut Crabs

Creeping Coconut Crabs

The coconut crab is a mysterious beast. It lives in the thick jungles of islands in the Indian and Pacific oceans. And it's one of the biggest crabs in the world. Coconut crabs can grow to be 3 feet long or more. They have ten legs. The back two legs are very small. The front two legs have big, strong claws. If you saw this crab, you might think it came from a scary movie.

But you probably *won't* see it. When the sun is out, the coconut crab likes to disappear. It prefers the shadows. It may come out if rain falls. But coconut crabs usually hide during the day. They dig into the sand or crawl between rocks.

The coconut crab also has other names, such as robber crab and palm thief. It earned these names by creeping into houses at night. Sometimes it eats food that it finds. Or it may steal shiny things like silverware or pans. The crab's raids are brave—and risky. When people find these big coconut crabs in their houses, they may hurt them.

Luckily, most of the time these crabs don't go into houses. Instead, they eat fruit and seeds in the jungle. Sometimes they climb coconut trees. They may use their claws to snip off the coconuts. When the fruit falls to the ground, sometimes it cracks open. But not always. The strong coconut crab can lift up to 60 pounds. So it might try to carry the coconut up the tree and drop it again. Or it may just use its claws to pound and pry open the shell. At last it gets to the sweet fruit inside.

The coconut crab has a great sense of smell. It can sniff out bananas and coconuts from far away. Sometimes the crabs eat dead animals or rotting plants. They've attacked rats and other small creatures. Some stories even say they have eaten people who were hurt or who had died.

But all creatures have weak spots. The coconut crab has rotten vision, and it can't swim. Plus, it seems to be ticklish. So if you spot a coconut crab in your home, you could toss it into a full bathtub or other water. But be very careful picking it up. If his strong claws clamp onto you, it'll hurt—a lot. And it's almost impossible to pry open those claws. There's a trick for getting them to let go, though. Gently tickle the crab on its soft tummy. Pretty soon, the critter will lose its hold. Whew!

From *Building Character with True Stories from Nature* by Barbara A. Lewis, copyright © 2012. Free Spirit Publishing Inc., Minneapolis, MN; 800-735-7323; www.freespirit.com. This page may be reproduced for use within an individual classroom. For all other uses, contact www.freespirit.com/company/permissions.cfm.

Talk It Over

Use these questions to guide your students in considering analogies between coconut crabs and perseverance, problem solving, and other character traits and behaviors in people.

Can you create an analogy between the coconut crab—which prefers to hunt in the darkness of night—and people who try to hide something?

- A person who fibs might try to cover up those lies with additional lies.

- During the day, coconut crabs sometimes hide under the sand. A person who has done something wrong might think that by hiding he or she can avoid responsibility or blame.

- When people don't feel confident, they sometimes try to hide their true personalities. They may lie to keep up the image they want. But most of the time, the truth comes out eventually.

Coconut Crab Facts

Coconut crabs don't just eat coconuts. They also use the husks to line their burrows.

Coconut crabs don't laugh, but they do loosen up when "tickled." For people, laughter is a healthful habit. Experts say that one minute of hearty laughter can provide heart rate benefits similar to a ten-minute workout.

During Charles Darwin's voyage on the *Beagle* in the 1830s, he saw coconut crabs on islands in the Indian Ocean. He described them as growing "to a monstrous size."

Sometimes coconut crabs go into people's homes to take shiny things that are appealing or interesting to them. This takes daring. If people catch the crabs in their homes, they may hurt them. Can you compare this to a human quality?

- It takes courage to speak out against injustice even when you're afraid.

- It can sometimes take courage to learn a new skill, or to perform in front of other people.

- It takes courage to tell the truth, especially if you know you might get in trouble for it.

- Many people stand up for what they believe in even when it's not popular. They have to be brave to stick to their values and be true to themselves.

The coconut crab is a good problem solver. Coconuts are very hard to crack open, but the crab keeps trying. Sometimes it takes a long time. Compare this to challenges that people face.

- If you keep trying to solve a math problem, you will eventually understand it better.

- If you keep practicing a talent that you want to develop, you will improve that talent over time.

- If you keep going even when things are tough, you will eventually see the rewards. Even if you don't succeed in the way you hoped to, you'll be building strong character muscles and learning new things.

The coconut crab does have weaknesses. It doesn't see well and it can't swim. And while it has very strong claws, it will let go when its stomach is tickled. What analogies can you make between these characteristics and human behavior?

- All people have weaknesses. It is important to accept people and to forgive them when they make mistakes.

- If you can imagine the results or consequences of a moment of weakness or of making a poor decision, you may be able to stop yourself or others from making that choice.

- Crabs let go when they are tickled, and laughter can also make people relax. Sometimes humor can lighten up a tense situation.

Activities

Activity 1: Models of Perseverance

Materials
None

Directions
Learn about people who have persevered and overcome challenges. You could investigate as a group, or ask students to write short individual reports and then share what they learn with the class. Talk about what it takes to persevere and what the rewards can be. The following subjects are examples of people kids might choose to study.

- Helen Keller lost her sight and hearing when she was nineteen months old. She became an educated woman and an author, and she spoke up for people with disabilities.

- Cyclist Lance Armstrong overcame cancer to win the Tour de France race seven times in a row.

- Winston Churchill overcame a stuttering problem and poor performance in school to become Prime Minister of the United Kingdom.

- Track star Jesse Owens won four gold medals at the 1936 Olympics in the face of racial prejudice.

- Bethany Hamilton, a surfer, lost her arm in a shark attack at the age of thirteen and went on to win a national surfing championship. Bethany's story was made into the movie *Soul Surfer.*

Activity 2: Why Lie?

Materials
Optional: Coconut crab picture (on CD-ROM)

Directions
Ask your class this question: **Why do people lie?**

Before answering aloud, have students write down some answers to this question. If desired, they could write on copies of the crab picture. Ask kids to try to come up with one answer for each of the crab's ten legs. Talk about how sometimes, when we aren't honest, our lies seem to have "legs" of their own. A lie can run away from us and cause big problems.

After kids have had some time to work, ask them to share their answers. Talk about their ideas and thoughts.

Possible answers: Fear of getting in trouble; to cover up an earlier lie; to impress someone; to damage someone else's reputation; because of insecurity; to pretend to be someone he or she is not; fear of the real truth; to get someone else in trouble; to embarrass someone; to avoid responsibility.

Activity 3: Words of Encouragement

Materials
Words of Encouragement handout (on CD-ROM)
Colored pencils or crayons

Directions
Ask kids to think about the example of Jason Lester. At the age of twelve, Jason was riding his bike when a car hit him. He was very badly injured, and his right arm was partially paralyzed. But he went on to be a talented and dedicated athlete, competing in high school baseball and football. As an adult, Jason became an Ironman competitor. In 2009, he won an ESPY Award for Best Male Athlete with a Disability. Jason's message to everyone is, "If you don't stop, you can't be stopped."

Pass out the handout. Invite kids to brainstorm messages and slogans that encourage perseverance. Here are some ideas to get kids started:

- When you are down, the only direction is up.
- You can do it!
- You never lose until you quit.
- Hard work builds strong character muscles.

When kids have chosen their slogans, have them write these sayings neatly on their handouts. If they like, they can decorate the forms with designs or drawings. Hang the slogans in your school. You could also ask permission to hang them in local stores, clubs, or faith communities. If you have budding musicians in your group, you could ask them to make one or more slogans into a song that your class could learn and perform.

Activity 4: Honesty Survey

Materials
None

Directions
Compose an honesty survey. Use the sample question below, or brainstorm a question as a group.

How often do you tell the truth?
(circle your answer)
Always • Most of the time • Sometimes • Never

Write or print the survey question on small strips of paper and give one to each student. Ask kids to hand in their answers anonymously.

Complete the survey of your classroom. Count the number of responses from each of the four categories. If desired, older students can do a math exercise by calculating the percentage of responses in each category.

Variation: Kids could also survey another class or their family members and report back.

Share the results of the honesty survey with your group. Be careful to avoid blaming or criticizing anyone. Discuss why it's sometimes difficult to be honest. Then talk about how we can work on being honest more of the time. Ask kids if they think it's ever appropriate or okay to lie. Discuss the challenges that can come up when honesty comes in conflict with another positive character trait or behavior, such as safety. For example, a student who is talking to a stranger on the phone might lie and say that her parent is home so that the caller won't know that she is alone. How do kids feel about this kind of conflict? How can we know what to do in situations like these?

Lesson 7
Crows

Character Key Words
Communication • Problem Solving • Respect • Tolerance and Acceptance •
Assertiveness

Students will
- learn interesting facts about crows, including their problem-solving skills and high intelligence
- make a connection between the crow's negative reputation to the way people sometimes label each other or make assumptions about others
- draw analogies between crows' communication and problem-solving skills and human behaviors
- relate the crow's cleanup activities to having respect for the different jobs that people do
- compare the aggressiveness that crows sometimes show to the bullying behavior that people may show

Overview
In some cultures, crows are associated with death and bad news. And these birds *do* have some unnerving traits. They eat carrion, have eerie calls, and sometimes attack people. But students will learn that the crow is also intelligent, good at solving problems, and a great communicator. And while the job of eating carrion may seem distasteful to us, it's also important for the health of our planet and its ecosystems. This information will help kids appreciate the fact that work that may not seem pleasant is still necessary and beneficial.

In addition, students can make an important connection between the sometimes aggressive actions of crows and bullying behavior in people. You can help your group use the story as a starting point for productive discussion about bullying and how to address it through respect, assertiveness, and other traits and behaviors.

Story
Clever Crows

Clever Crows

One day, a man named Shimshon heard squawking outside his home. A baby crow had fallen out of its nest. Shimshon was annoyed with its loud caws. So he picked up the chick and carried it outside his garden. "Problem solved," he thought.

Big mistake.

Suddenly a large mother crow swooped down. She attacked Shimshon's head over and over. He finally ran inside. But the crow wasn't done with him. Every time Shimshon left his house, she dived at him again. He started wearing a helmet and carrying an umbrella whenever he went outside.

Then Shimshon noticed something odd. The crow never bothered his wife or kids. What was going on?

Bird experts have the answer. They have discovered something amazing. All crows look the same to most people. But we don't all look the same to crows. They can recognize human faces.

Like most animals, crows are very protective of their babies. So Shimshon was in trouble when he moved the crow chick.

Crows have good memories, too. And they communicate. They warn each other about danger. If one crow is killed in a farmer's field, the whole flock may avoid the place for two years.

Here's a strange crow habit. Sometimes they peck at windows and mirrors. This happens because male crows want to protect their nests and families. When a male crow sees his reflection, he gets confused. He thinks it's another bird on his turf. He can peck so hard at the reflection that he hurts himself.

You might not think this sounds very smart. But crows are some of the brightest birds around. They're curious and playful. Some can mimic human voices.

From *Building Character with True Stories from Nature* by Barbara A. Lewis, copyright © 2012. Free Spirit Publishing Inc., Minneapolis, MN; 800-735-7323; www.freespirit.com. This page may be reproduced for use within an individual classroom. For all other uses, contact www.freespirit.com/company/permissions.cfm.

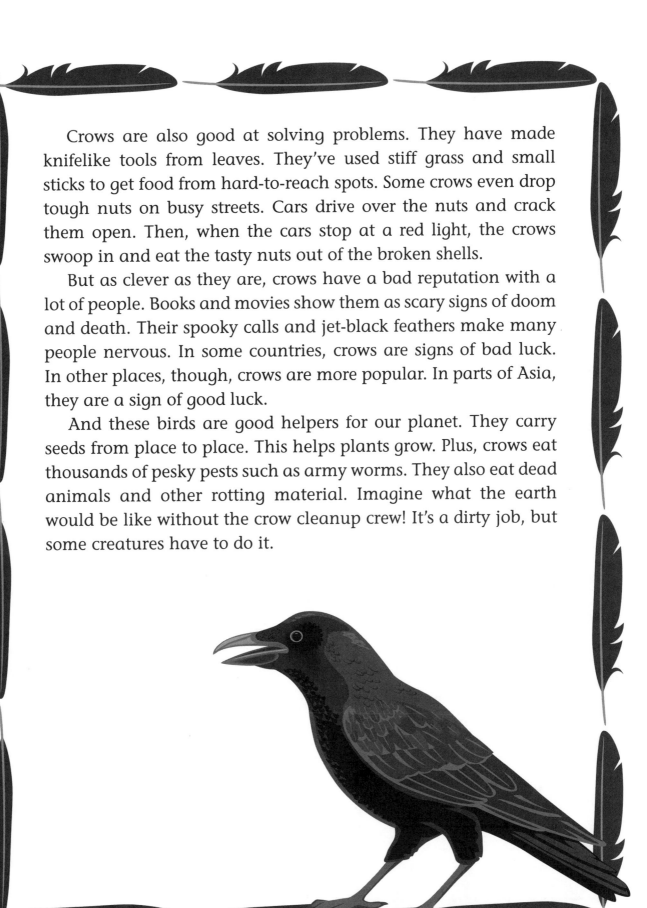

Crows are also good at solving problems. They have made knifelike tools from leaves. They've used stiff grass and small sticks to get food from hard-to-reach spots. Some crows even drop tough nuts on busy streets. Cars drive over the nuts and crack them open. Then, when the cars stop at a red light, the crows swoop in and eat the tasty nuts out of the broken shells.

But as clever as they are, crows have a bad reputation with a lot of people. Books and movies show them as scary signs of doom and death. Their spooky calls and jet-black feathers make many people nervous. In some countries, crows are signs of bad luck. In other places, though, crows are more popular. In parts of Asia, they are a sign of good luck.

And these birds are good helpers for our planet. They carry seeds from place to place. This helps plants grow. Plus, crows eat thousands of pesky pests such as army worms. They also eat dead animals and other rotting material. Imagine what the earth would be like without the crow cleanup crew! It's a dirty job, but some creatures have to do it.

From *Building Character with True Stories from Nature* by Barbara A. Lewis, copyright © 2012. Free Spirit Publishing Inc., Minneapolis, MN; 800-735-7323; www.freespirit.com. This page may be reproduced for use within an individual classroom. For all other uses, contact www.freespirit.com/company/permissions.cfm.

Talk It Over

Use these questions to guide your students in considering analogies between crows and assertiveness, communication, and other character traits and behaviors in people.

Sometimes crows attack people they see as threats. Can you make a comparison with people who bully others?

- Crows usually attack because they think the person is an enemy. Maybe some people who bully see other people as enemies.

- Sometimes bullying happens because kids don't understand each other, or because they feel afraid.

- People who bully may pick on people who they think are weak and won't fight back. If you see bullying happen, be calm but assertive with the person who is bullying. You could say, "No bullying allowed." If you don't feel safe, get away from the situation. And always tell an adult if you are bullied or if someone else is being bullied.

Crow Facts

Crows communicate using more than 200 different calls.

A crow that attacks its own image calls to mind the famous line from Walt Kelly's *Pogo* comic strip: "We have met the enemy and he is us."

Crows have tightly knit family systems. Young crows may stay with their parents for several years and even help care for younger siblings.

Male crows sometimes attack their own reflections in windows or mirrors. What do people do that is similar to this behavior?

- Sometimes it's easier to blame others for our problems than it is to think that we might be partly responsible for them.

- When a crow attacks his image in a mirror, he can hurt his own beak. When we are unkind to others, we hurt ourselves, as well. We feel bad later. We can damage friendships. And we can lessen the respect that other people have for us.

- We might not admit when we've made mistakes because we don't want other people to think that we aren't smart. But it's important to take responsibility for our own actions, even when we make mistakes.

Crows are great problem solvers. Can you think of ways that people solve problems?

- Working together on a problem can make it easier.

- Some problems are really tough. But if we keep trying, we'll make progress.

- Using your imagination is a big help when you're trying to solve a problem. It can spark new ideas and creative solutions.

Crows are good at communicating with each other. When they know of a danger, they warn other crows. How is communication important for people?

- Communication makes relationships stronger. It brings people closer together.

- Sometimes people talk without truly communicating. Real communication requires good listening and understanding.

- When we see something that makes us nervous or afraid, it helps to tell someone about it. Telling someone can help us stay safe.

- Communication is necessary between groups of people, such as communities and countries. Good communication can help create understanding and peace.

People in some parts of the world believe that crows are bad luck, while others think they bring good fortune. Can you think of ways this idea relates to how people see each other?

- People have all kinds of different beliefs, traditions, and ideas. New ideas might seem strange to us at first, but different ideas make the world interesting.

- We should always respect other people's ideas, even if they're not the same as ours.

Crows are nature's cleanup crew. They eat dead animals, even when they're starting to rot. That might sound gross, but it's good for our planet. Can you make an analogy with this idea?

- People do many different jobs. Not all jobs sound good to everyone. But all of them are valuable to our community and our world in some way. It's important to appreciate and respect the jobs that people do.

- Sometimes we all have chores and other jobs that we'd rather not do. But doing these things—like cleaning your room, helping make dinner, or taking care of a brother or sister—makes our lives better and helps others.

- All animals play important roles in nature. All people are important, too. Everyone's work has value.

Activities

Activity 1: The Lemon Game

Materials
Tennis balls (4 or 5)
Permanent marker

Directions
Before playing the game, use a permanent marker to draw symbols—a circle, square, star, and so forth—on several tennis balls. These symbols will remind you what each ball represents.

Have everyone stand or sit in a circle. Pass one tennis ball to the student on your right and say, "This is a lemon." That first student then passes the tennis ball to the next student and repeats, "This is a lemon." This continues around the circle.

After two or three students have passed the first tennis ball, each making the above statement as they present the tennis ball to the next person on their right, introduce a second ball to the circle. This time, say, "This is a jelly bean."

Continue to pass out the rest of the tennis balls, calling each one by a false name.

Then, once all the balls are being passed around the circle, say, "Reverse." Instruct kids to pass the balls in the opposite direction now, each one restating the name that was given for each ball. You can reverse the direction as many times as you like. The game continues until most students are confused about what each tennis ball is supposed to be, and the laughter begins.

Follow the game with a conversation about open-mindedness, bullying behavior, and honest communication. Opening prompts might include the following:

- Just saying that a tennis ball is a lemon doesn't make it a lemon. And calling a person an unkind name doesn't make that name true.

- It's unfair to make assumptions about people or label them. Every person has many sides to his or her character.

- If you don't communicate honestly with others, you might start to feel confused about your true ideas and values. It's hard to remember a lie and keep it straight.

Activity 2: In Harmony

Materials
Optional: Sheet music for one or more songs
Optional: CD player or musical instrument(s)

Directions
Teach your students a song about assertiveness, conflict resolution, or ways to reduce bullying. If you are interested in purchasing music, you can find lyrics and music to songs such as "I Can Talk It Out,"

"Conflict Resolution Helps You Find the Very Best Solution," and "Bully-Proof Our School" at www.songsforteaching.com/charactereducationsongs.htm. Otherwise, write an original song with your class. If desired, you could provide simple instruments for students to play. Encourage kids to think about respectful and productive ways to resolve disagreements and address bullying. Talk about how conflict and bullying reduce harmony in your classroom.

Activity 3: All Mixed Up

Materials

All Mixed Up handout (on CD-ROM)

Directions

Hand out copies of the All Mixed Up handout. (*Note:* There are two versions of this handout with different degrees of difficulty. Use one or both, depending on the needs of your group. The answers follow below.) Remind kids that crows are good at problem solving. Explain how anagrams work and do an example together if desired.

Then give kids some time to work on the puzzles. Afterward, talk about what kids found challenging, fun, or surprising about this activity. Discuss how problem solving can be a helpful skill, and brainstorm strategies for approaching a challenging problem.

All Mixed Up answers:

Simpler handout:

RWCO = CROW

WCA = CAW

PSREETC = RESPECT

VLOES = SOLVE

PEKE YRNIGT = KEEP TRYING

More difficult handout:

MICNEUOTMAC = COMMUNICATE

NOLERECTA = TOLERANCE

CENECCATPA = ACCEPTANCE

BPRLOME LNOISVG = PROBLEM SOLVING

ON BNLLUGIY EADWLLO = NO BULLYING ALLOWED

Activity 4: Being Honest About Bullying

Materials

Journals

Directions

Invite students to write in their journals about bullying. If they need help getting started, suggest the following questions to think about:

- Have you had any experiences with bullying?

- What are some positive ways to respond to bullying?

- How can we reduce bullying at our school?

After kids have had some time to write, lead a discussion on what the students think about bullying and how to reduce it. As a group, brainstorm a list of ideas and guidelines for reducing and responding to bullying. When you have a good list, make it into a chart or poster and display it in your classroom.

Lesson 8
Cuttlefish

Character Key Words
Honesty • Integrity • Adaptability • Tolerance and Acceptance

Students will
- learn interesting facts about cuttlefish, including their amazing camouflaging skill
- compare the cuttlefish's ability to change its appearance to the way people sometimes change aspects of themselves—such as their language, behavior, or dress—depending on the people who are around them
- think about how staying true to yourself and being consistent in your good behavior is part of integrity
- draw analogies between the cuttlefish's adaptability and people who adapt to new situations

Overview
Your students face deception and dishonesty in many aspects of their lives, from false advertisements to people who hide their true character. Being able to think critically and to tell truth from falsehoods are important skills that will serve your students well as they grow and as they explore the world. The cuttlefish lesson provides a starting point for conversation about these ideas, as well as an exploration of being true to oneself and developing personal integrity. (*Note:* Integrity can be a tricky concept for younger kids to grasp, so you may want to have a discussion about this character trait before you get into the details of this lesson.)

Story
The Not-So-Cuddly Cuttlefish

The Not-So-Cuddly Cuttlefish

Cuttlefish. The name sounds . . . well . . . cuddly! Maybe you think you'd like to have a cuttlefish as a pet. But what would happen if you put it in an aquarium with other fish? Chances are, your goldfish and guppies would begin to disappear. Cuttlefish eat little fish, crabs, and shrimp.

The cuttlefish's name is a little confusing. Cuttlefish aren't really fish at all. They're mollusks. Mollusks have soft bodies and no backbone. Many of them have hard outer shells. But not the cuttlefish. Its shell is inside. It's called the cuttlebone. This hollow bone has many little spaces in it. The cuttlefish moves up or down in the water by filling or emptying these spaces with gas.

And cuttlefish aren't cuddly. In fact, many of them are poisonous. They have toxins in their saliva and muscles. Cuttlefish don't have hard shells to protect them from predators. So their poison helps protect them from animals that want to eat them.

Cuttlefish also have other ways to stay safe. They're masters of disguise, like spies of the sea. When in danger, a cuttlefish sprays a cloud of black liquid into the water. This liquid is called ink. While the hungry predator fumbles in the darkness, the cuttlefish sneaks away.

And that's not all. Move over, chameleons! Many cuttlefish have an amazing ability. They can change their colors and patterns. They can even change texture and shape. When they sense danger, they quickly blend in with the background. They hide in plain sight.

The Pfeffer's flamboyant cuttlefish doesn't blend in. Instead, it puts on a wild display. It flashes quickly from one color to the next. One moment it's bright red. Suddenly it's neon yellow. This colorful show sends a message. *Don't you dare eat me. I'm poisonous. Stay back.*

Some cuttlefish use their camouflage skills to find partners. Small males sometimes disguise themselves as females. They change their color and pattern to match the way females look. Then they slip past bigger males and mate with females. Pretty sneaky!

From *Building Character with True Stories from Nature* by Barbara A. Lewis, copyright © 2012. Free Spirit Publishing Inc., Minneapolis, MN; 800-735-7323; www.freespirit.com. This page may be reproduced for use within an individual classroom. For all other uses, contact www.freespirit.com/company/permissions.cfm.

Talk It Over

Use these questions to guide your students in considering analogies between cuttlefish and honesty, adaptability, and other character traits and behaviors in people.

Cuttlefish change color and texture to trick others—both predators and mates. Sometimes people also seem to change depending on where they are or what people they are with. Can you think of examples of this?

- People are not always exactly who they seem to be. For example, they might lie to make themselves seem important or to avoid trouble.

- A person might dress a certain way because he or she wants to impress others.

- Sometimes kids use bad words when they are around certain friends but use different language when they are around their family or teachers.

- Some kids play violent video games or watch movies that are for grown-ups but tell their parents that they don't. You should always be trustworthy in the things that you do and claim to be.

The cuttlefish changes its appearance to stay safe. But when people pretend to be something they are not, it can hurt them, because it damages their integrity. Showing integrity means that your actions and your values match. Why is it important to show integrity? When can it be hard to do this?

- When your actions and beliefs don't match, you might feel uncomfortable or unhappy. Integrity feels better.

- If you try to have too many different identities, you might start to get mixed up. You can feel like you forget who you really are and what you really care about.

- Sometimes people might tease you for standing up for your beliefs.

- Sometimes your friends might want you to do something that goes against your values. It can be hard to choose between being with your friends and staying true to yourself.

The cuttlefish can change its appearance to fool others. Can you think of things in people's lives that might fool them?

- Commercials and other ads might tell you something that is not true. For example, an ad might say, "It's the best product money can buy!" But is it really the best? It's important to think carefully about what you see, read, and hear, and to draw your own conclusions.

- Sometimes we are fooled by stereotypes. We think that all people from certain groups are alike. But instead, we should decide what people are like by getting to know them and by watching their behavior. It's not a good idea to assume all people are the same.

Cuttlefish Facts

The cuttlefish has three hearts and blue-green blood.

To move through the water, a cuttlefish uses a method similar to jet propulsion. It pulls water into its mantle cavity and then shoots it out with great force. The way cuttlefish control their buoyancy is similar to how submarines operate.

Cuttlefish ink was the original source of the sepia dye used by artists.

The cuttlefish uses poison, camouflage, and ink to keep predators at a distance. How do you think people sometimes keep others at a distance? Why do you think they might do this?

- A person might speak harshly or act unkindly to keep other people away. This could be because he or she is embarrassed about something or doesn't feel good about himself or herself.

- A person who seems unfriendly might actually just be shy or not know how to make friends.

- Some people who have had their feelings hurt in the past might be afraid of making close friends. They might be worried about being hurt again by people they care about.

The cuttlefish doesn't have a hard outside shell to protect it. Instead, it has other ways of surviving, such as changing color and spraying ink. Can you compare this to people who have to adapt to new or different situations?

- People who have health problems that prevent them from doing some activities can still do great things. For example, Stephen Hawking has a disease that has made him unable to move or to talk. But he is one of the most famous scientists in the world.

- Kids who don't have the size or strength to do one sport can learn another one. For example, if you're not tall enough to play basketball, you might try swimming, golf, or some other sport.

- People who have allergies to certain foods must learn to eat other foods instead. This can be hard, especially if they really like the foods they can't eat anymore. But they'll feel better if they stick to the foods that are good for them.

Activities

Activity 1: A Story of Deception

Materials
Chart paper, board, or other surface for composing the story

Markers or chalk

Directions
Write a group story about someone who lies or deceives others. Describe how one lie might lead to another. Try to guide the story to include a change of behavior when the character learns to be true to others and to himself or herself. It may take kids a while to get warmed up, so before the activity, compose a few prompts that you can use to get the storytelling started—and also, if necessary, to keep the story creation on track. For example, **What should we name our character? What does the character do next? How do you think this makes the character feel?**

Invite students to raise their hands to add different points and developments to the tale. The story could be funny or serious. Afterward, talk with kids about the story and how it developed. What ways could the story have gone differently? How can we write our own stories as we live our lives? Could deciding to lie—or not lie—in one situation have an effect on things that happen later on?

Activity 2: Master of Disguise

Materials
Drawing paper

Markers, pencils, crayons, paints

Optional: Printouts of cuttlefish picture (on CD-ROM)

Directions
Have kids draw a cuttlefish in hiding. They might choose a cuttlefish that's pretending to look like sand, a plant, or some other background. (If you like, search the Internet for images of cuttlefish in camouflage and show them to your students. Kids will be amazed by what cuttlefish can do.)

Variation: If younger students find it too challenging to draw their own cuttlefish, you can hand out copies of the cuttlefish picture and ask kids to color it with lots of bright colors like the Pfeffer's flamboyant cuttlefish.

When kids have finished their pictures, invite them to show the class. Talk about the ways people sometimes try to blend in with the background, like a hiding cuttlefish—or how they might try to stand out, like the colorful Pfeffer's flamboyant cuttlefish. Why do some people like to go unnoticed? Why do others prefer to be in the spotlight? (Be sure to guide this conversation carefully to keep it from getting personal about anyone in the class.)

Activity 3: Many Talents

Materials

Various

Directions

Hold a classroom talent showcase. Kids who want to perform can do so, while others can submit drawings, writings, or other work. If some kids' talents are sports or something else that can't be performed in class, ask them to share pictures of them doing these activities or to write stories about them. You could create a display space in your room for all of these contributions, or put together a booklet and make copies that kids can take home.

After the showcase, talk about how we all have different talents. No one is good at everything, and everyone is good at something. If some kids developed their talents because they were unable to do some other activity, invite them to share this information, but be clear that it's voluntary. Ask kids to think about what they would do instead of the talent they chose to showcase, if for some reason they couldn't have that talent anymore. Again, ask them to share their thoughts if they feel comfortable doing so.

Activity 4: Turning Off the Heat

Materials

Heat-resistant glass flask with a narrow neck
Water
Balloon (8-inch round balloons work best)
Safety glasses
Hot plate or other heating unit
Hot pads or oven mitts
Optional: Shallow dish of ice water

Directions

Put a few tablespoons of water into the flask. Then place the balloon over the neck of the bottle or flask. Put on your safety glasses, and place the bottle on the hot plate. Slowly begin to heat the flask until the water boils and creates vapor. As the air and vapor heat up, their molecules spread out and bounce around more rapidly. The warming air takes up more space, moving and causing it to expand. Once the balloon has filled up a bit, turn off the hot plate.

Use a hot pad to remove the flask from the heating unit. Place the flask on a second hot pad.

As you do this experiment, talk with kids about the way dishonesty and deception can be like the balloon as the water heats up. Lies can grow and grow. Tell kids that if the air inside the bottle keeps heating up, the balloon could eventually pop. Similarly, when people find out that someone has been dishonest, their respect for and trust in that person can "pop." Ask kids to think about how to "turn off the heat" when they are being dishonest or pretending to be someone else. Be honest about the fact that this can be difficult. Is it hard to be ourselves sometimes? Is it tempting to lie? Why is it better to tell the truth?

Variation: After the balloon expands, move the flask from the heating surface to a dish of ice water. The water vapor in the flask and balloon will quickly condense, creating a partial vacuum. The greater air pressure outside will push the balloon into the flask. You could compare this to submitting to pressure from others to lie. Ask kids what other analogies they see between this phenomenon and honesty and integrity.

Lesson 9
Dandelions

Character Key Words
Hard Work • Problem Solving • Citizenship • Tolerance and Acceptance

Students will
- learn some facts about dandelions, including their rapid growth and their different uses throughout history and around the world
- discuss the importance of problem solving and hard work in finding solutions
- consider how looking at a situation in a new way or from a different perspective can change your ideas about it and can lead to greater tolerance and acceptance
- compare dandelions' quick spread with human behavior that can grow out of control
- draw an analogy between the dandelion's deep roots and citizenship

Overview
Dandelions have a bad reputation in the United States. Their aggressive spread across lawns and their ability to adapt have made them Public Enemy #1 for many gardeners. But in many parts of the world, they are valued as a food crop and a source of medicine. Through the story, you can help kids understand the analogy that sometimes we have false perceptions of a problem or of other people, and that our views vary depending on where we live and what information we have. Learning more about something or someone can help us understand situations better and from a new point of view.

Your students can also explore the idea that, like the dandelion's rapid growth, certain behaviors can spread very quickly, such as telling rumors. The results can be damaging and hard to undo. On the other hand, kindness, good manners, honesty, dependability, and other positive traits can also spread from person to person.

Story
Determined Dandelions

Determined Dandelions

It's a beautiful springtime Saturday. You have plans with your friends. But your dad has a different idea. He says you're in charge of destroying dandelions in the yard. And, he adds, "Be sure to dig down to the root. Otherwise, those little yellow heads will be back before we know it."

So much for having fun. You crawl across the grass for hours. As you dig and pull, you pretend you're in a battle. You make explosion sounds as you rip out each dandelion. "Kaboom! Another one bites the dust." When you finish, there are no dandelions to be seen. You're proud of your work. But you also feel a little sad for the cheerful flowers.

Three days later, your dad sees a fluffy yellow blossom on the lawn. Then he spots another. And another. You remind your dad that you already did your job. But he just smiles and hands you the weed digger.

You sigh. "My work will never be done!" You don't feel sorry for the dandelions anymore. You just want them gone. You attack the flowers with a growl. You have to get them before those white fluff balls appear. They look soft and harmless. But they are collections of tiny parachutes. As these parachutes float away, they spread dandelion seeds. And each dandelion head has 150 to 200 seeds. You decide you'll never again blow dandelion fluff across your yard.

Finally, you're sure you got them all. The grass will be safe from the dandelion invasion until your family gets back from your summer trip. Right?

Wrong. While you're gone, a few new yellow heads pop up. They draw bees like magnets. Bees just can't stay away from dandelion nectar. The bright beautiful yellow flowers burst into fluffy white balls. They scatter seeds all over your lawn.

From *Building Character with True Stories from Nature* by Barbara A. Lewis, copyright © 2012. Free Spirit Publishing Inc., Minneapolis, MN; 800-735-7323; www.freespirit.com. This page may be reproduced for use within an individual classroom. For all other uses, contact www.freespirit.com/company/permissions.cfm.

You get home to a field of dandelions with tufts of grass growing between them. Your grassy yard has turned yellow with "lions." You decide this calls for all-out warfare. You grab a hammer from your dad's toolbox and stomp outside. You smash the flowers. "Take that! Bam!" But pretty soon your arm hurts. And you have a feeling the dandelions will still be back.

Next, your dad brings home an armful of library books. He says that there must be a way to beat the dandelions. Together, you read and plan your attack.

To your surprise, you learn that many people don't *want* to get rid of dandelions. In plenty of places around the world, dandelions are food. You read a legend about the island of Minorca, near Spain. Hundreds of years ago, the story goes, a huge swarm of locusts landed on the island. They ate up all the crops. But the islanders survived—thanks to dandelions. They dug up the roots and ate them until the locusts were gone.

You also find out that dandelions are good for you. The roots, leaves, and flowers have all kinds of healthful vitamins and minerals. People in Europe toss the greens into their salads. They eat the roots as veggies. Some people drink dandelion tea.

And that's not all. For centuries, Chinese people have used dandelions to treat sicknesses. So have some Native Americans. Dandelions might be one of nature's super foods.

Your dad closes the book. "In the end, nature always wins," he says. You remind your dad that you *told* him digging up dandelions was a waste of time. He laughs. The war is over. Next spring, you won't bother fighting. You'll trade your garden fork for a salad fork. Then you'll relax and watch for a new crop of dandelions to enjoy.

From *Building Character with True Stories from Nature* by Barbara A. Lewis, copyright © 2012. Free Spirit Publishing Inc., Minneapolis, MN; 800-735-7323; www.freespirit.com. This page may be reproduced for use within an individual classroom. For all other uses, contact www.freespirit.com/company/permissions.cfm.

Talk It Over

Use these questions to guide your students in considering analogies between dandelions and character traits and behaviors in people.

Dandelions can spread very quickly if gardeners don't stop them early enough. Can you think of anything in your life that can get out of control if you're not careful?

- If you put off doing your homework for too long, or if you don't do some assignments, you can quickly fall way behind.

- If you lie a lot, things can get out of control.

- If you don't do your chores, they can pile up and get overwhelming.

- Rumors and gossip can spread very quickly.

- If you do kind things for others, that can spread fast, too. People who are treated nicely often feel like doing nice things for others.

- Illness can spread fast. Washing your hands and staying home when you are sick can help slow down or even prevent the spread of colds and other illnesses.

The kid in "Determined Dandelions" felt that trying to get rid of the dandelions was a waste of time and energy. Are there some things that you do—or that other people do—that seem like wasted effort, that never seem to get done, or that you don't want to do?

- Holding a grudge or staying mad for a long time wastes your energy. It can make you feel bad and keep you from having fun.

- Sometimes homework isn't fun. But it's important to keep up with your schoolwork so that you learn and keep your mind busy and sharp.

- Some chores, like washing the dishes or cleaning your room, might seem pointless to you sometimes. After all, dishes just get dirty again, and your room probably will, too. But helping with these jobs makes your home nicer for everybody.

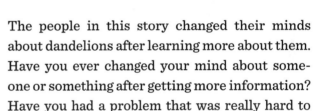

Dandelion Facts

Dandelion roots, leaves, and flowers have vitamins including A, C, and K, as well as many minerals.

Dandelion root is a traditional ingredient in some kinds of root beer.

The name *dandelion* comes from French for "lion's tooth."

The people in this story changed their minds about dandelions after learning more about them. Have you ever changed your mind about someone or something after getting more information? Have you had a problem that was really hard to solve until you looked at it in a different way?

- If you believe something is true, and then you get more information from someone who sees things differently, you might change your mind.

- When problems happen, you often have to learn to adapt to new situations and find new ways of working things out.

- When you're doing homework, you may not understand it at first. But if you get help or look up more information, you might start to see the answers more clearly.

- Sometimes people think or say unkind things about people they don't know or who are different from them. But when people get to know other people, they understand them better. They might even become friends. It's best not to make assumptions about others.

Dandelions' long roots make them strong. These roots are part of what makes them so difficult to get rid of. People have "roots," too. We have ties to our families, communities, schools, and other groups. Citizenship means being part of these groups. What are some ways to be a good citizen?

- Learning about how your government works

- Helping other people in the community

- Respecting and following the rules of your community, classroom, or family

- Helping keep your school, neighborhood, or town clean and safe

Activities

Activity 1: How Does Your Garden Grow?

Materials

Long planter or several tall pots

Potting soil or dirt

Dandelion seeds (you can buy these or harvest them from fluffy dandelion heads)

Water

Directions

With kids' help, fill the planter or pots with potting soil or dirt, leaving about an inch at the top of the container. Plant the seeds in the dirt, burying them about ¼ to ½ inch deep .

Put the planter or pots somewhere in your room that gets as much sunlight as possible. If you don't have a sunny spot, see if you can put the plants in some other part of your school.

Keep the soil moist. Invite kids to take turns watering the growing dandelions.

Over the next couple of weeks, check in on your dandelion plants regularly. Talk with students about what plants need to grow, such as light, water, and soil. Discuss how people also need certain things to grow and be healthy. For example, exercise and nutritious food are important for keeping our bodies healthy and strong. Learning and being curious help our minds stay sharp and active.

Once you have a crop of dandelions, pull up one of the flowers. Show kids the taproot, and explain that it can be more than a foot long in a full-grown plant. This is part of what makes it so hard to get rid of dandelions. Talk with kids about how people also have "roots." Being a good citizen and having strong connections to our families, friends, schools, and communities can help us be healthy and happy.

Variation: Get parents' permission to send some dandelion greens home with kids for their families to try in a dish. Make sure to choose young, tender greens. Dandelion greens get bitter as they age.

Activity 2: Dandelion Words

Materials

None

Directions

Have students write articles, stories, or poems about dandelions. Ask them to compare or contrast dandelions and their characteristics to human traits and behaviors, such as determination, problem solving, acceptance, and hard work. If you like, hold an in-class workshop to help kids revise and polish their writing. Then encourage them to submit their pieces to the school paper or literary journal, or to a community newsletter. Or, compile the writings in a booklet and send it home with kids to share with their friends and families.

Activity 3: Survey Says . . .

Materials

Dandelion Survey handout (on CD-ROM)

Directions

Conduct a survey to find out how people feel about dandelions. How popular—or unpopular—are they? As a group, come up with two to five questions, depending on the age of your group. Sample questions might include:

- Do your families dig up dandelions, or do they ignore them?

- Have you ever tasted a dandelion green?

- Do you think dandelions are pretty or just pesky?

Enter your chosen questions on the customizable Dandelion Survey handout and give every student two copies of the survey form. Then pair up kids and have them survey each other. In addition, ask them each to survey one person outside of school.

When kids have gathered all the answers, help them use the data to calculate fractions or percentages reflecting the information they collected. *Example:* Three-fourths (or 75 percent) of the people surveyed have never eaten a dandelion green. (Younger students can phrase these values as "Three out of four people...")

Talk with your class about what they learned. How hard or easy is it to change people's opinions? Did students' own opinions change at all in the course of the survey?

Lesson 10
Dogs

Character Key Words
Caring • Friendship • Loyalty • Courage • Service • Forgiveness • Responsibility

Students will
- learn some interesting characteristics about dogs, including their courage, service, and caring, and make analogies to these traits among people
- compare the loyalty that dogs display to human behavior
- think about the friendship and forgiveness that dogs seem to show toward people and compare these traits to similar qualities in people
- consider the many jobs dogs do for humans, and compare this to ideas of service and responsibility among people

Overview
The friendship that connects dogs and people provides an example of loyalty, caring, and dedication. Kids will enjoy talking about these traits in dogs and making connections to human actions, relationships, and behavior. Examples of dogs' service and courage can also provide a great starting point for conversations about helping others.

In addition, many of your students may have dogs, or have friends or neighbors who do. They will probably be eager to share stories about the dogs they know. You might discuss how the way that people treat their dogs can affect these pets' loyalty or friendship, and draw an analogy to how our treatment of other people affects our relationships with them.

Story
Loyal Dogs

Loyal Dogs

Every morning, Hachiko wagged his tail good-bye as his owner left for work. Hachiko was a fluffy brown Akita dog. His owner was a professor at the University of Tokyo in Japan. The professor took the train to his job. Each afternoon, when the professor got off the train, Hachiko was waiting at the station.

But one day, the professor didn't come home. He had died suddenly. A new owner adopted Hachiko. But the dog missed the professor. For nine years, loyal Hachiko kept going to the train station. He didn't understand that his beloved master was gone. So he waited and waited.

People at the station noticed Hachiko. His faithfulness impressed them. They fed him. They patted him and said hello when they passed.

Years later, Hachiko died. But people didn't forget him, just as he never forgot the professor. Today, if you go to the Shibuya train station, you'll see a statue of Hachiko. People pat the statue and touch its paws. They use the statue as a meeting spot. Sometimes they put flowers, blankets, or other little gifts on it. Every year, a ceremony honors Hachiko's memory.

Hachiko's dedication was extra special. But many dogs have very close bonds with people. They play with us. They cuddle. And they also work with us. Many dogs have jobs. Some guard buildings. Some work with police. Others go to war with soldiers.

Some working dogs guide people who are blind or deaf. Others help kids and adults with autism. Some dogs help elderly people or people with injuries.

Rescue dogs have saved people from all kinds of dangers. They've guided people through snowstorms. Dogs have even saved people from pirates and alligators! They've also pulled people out of fallen buildings. That's what a police dog named Trakr did.

On September 11, 2001, terrorists attacked the World Trade Center in New York City. The two towers fell in piles of rubble. Many people were trapped. Trakr, a German shepherd, was a police dog from Nova

From *Building Character with True Stories from Nature* by Barbara A. Lewis, copyright © 2012. Free Spirit Publishing Inc., Minneapolis, MN; 800-735-7323; www.freespirit.com. This page may be reproduced for use within an individual classroom. For all other uses, contact www.freespirit.com/company/permissions.cfm.

Scotia, Canada. He was loyal and brave, even in a very scary situation. He helped dig through thirty feet of dangerous debris to find a missing person. Trakr could have died. But he found the last survivor of the attack and helped save her.

Later, Trakr got sick. He couldn't use his back legs anymore. Some people think the smoke from the World Trade Center made him sick. Even after Trakr died, people remembered his courage and service. Scientists wanted to clone a dog. Cloning is like making a copy. Scientists have learned how to clone animals by using some of their cells. People decided that brave Trakr was a great dog to clone. Now there are five young dogs that look just like Trakr. They have his brave heart. They're learning to be rescue dogs like him.

With their loyalty and courage, dogs have earned the friendship of people around the world. Most dogs don't lead lives as dramatic as those of Hachiko or Trakr. But their love and warmth are still important. Dogs don't care what you look like. They accept you as you are. Maybe you had a bad day at school. Or you got into an argument with a friend. Maybe you made a mistake. Your dog puts his paws on your chest. He licks the tears from your face. He nuzzles your hand. And suddenly, you feel a little bit better. Your dog really might be your best friend.

From *Building Character with True Stories from Nature* by Barbara A. Lewis, copyright © 2012. Free Spirit Publishing Inc., Minneapolis, MN; 800-735-7323; www.freespirit.com. This page may be reproduced for use within an individual classroom. For all other uses, contact www.freespirit.com/company/permissions.cfm.

Talk It Over

Use these questions to guide your students in considering analogies between dogs and courage, service, and other character traits and behaviors in people.

Hachiko stayed loyal to his owner long after the professor died. Sometimes people are sad for a very long time over the loss of someone or something they loved. Can this be helpful? Can it ever be harmful?

- Losing someone or something can cause you to think carefully about the way you feel and the things you think are important. Sometimes hard times and sadness can help us become stronger people. We can learn from what we've gone through.

- Different kinds of loss can make us sad. Sometimes when we move to a new home, switch schools, or go through another big change, we feel like we've lost something. These changes can be hard at first, but usually, over time, we begin to feel better.

- Mourning the loss of someone or something can help you be more understanding for other people in similar situations. Your own experience can make you better able to comfort others.

- It's normal and healthy to feel sad when we lose someone or something we love. But sometimes, being very sad for a very long time can keep people from moving on with their lives.

Dogs seem to like helping people and working with them. Do people gain happiness from serving other people or causes? Do you think service can be good for the people *doing* the service? In what ways might that happen?

- Doing service for others can make other people's lives better. At the same time, it can make the person doing the service feel needed and valued.

- Doing service feels good. Helping others makes us happy.

- Service can get you more involved and interested in your community. It can also help you meet people and make new friends.

- Serving others can give you a better understanding of what is important to you. It can help you learn how you want to live your life.

- *Note:* If desired, you can share this information with students and talk about it with them: Many students who get involved in service projects end up with better attitudes, higher self-esteem, improved grades and ability to use higher-level thinking skills, and increased school attendance. Serving others and volunteering can also result in health benefits. Researchers have found that it can lead to longer lives and lower rates of depression.

Dogs are usually very loyal to their owners. People can be loyal to each other, too. How is loyalty helpful?

- When people feel loyal to their friends, school, neighborhoods, faith communities, or other groups, they are more likely to help the group. They will feel involved and cared about.

- When people are loyal to a group, they often grow to care about the other members of that group. They want to help each other. In return, they get support and help from other people in the group.

- When a person is loyal to you, that loyalty can help you feel safe and secure.

Dogs seem to show forgiving behaviors. How does it feel when you forgive others? What about when you don't forgive?

- Holding a grudge against someone can make you feel miserable. It can even make you sick. But when you forgive, you can move on. You feel better and happier.

- Forgiving other people can sometimes change their behavior. They may think about what they did to hurt someone else and decide to be kinder in the future. And if they've been feeling bad about themselves, being forgiven by the people they hurt can help them forgive themselves, too.

- If you don't forgive, your anger and hurt can get worse. Your feelings can grow into a bigger problem.

Sometimes dogs rescue people. The have even helped other species, including cats, which are often thought of as rivals of dogs. People naturally help people they love and those with common goals. **What might you learn from the example of a dog's caring?**

- As humans, we are all more alike than we are different, even if on the surface we don't seem to have much in common.

- All people who have needs deserve to be helped by others who can offer assistance and care.

- Helping others can help you find out new things about yourself. You might learn more about what you value, what you care about, or what you like to do with your time.

Dog Facts

The dog name *Fido* comes from Latin and means "to trust" or "to believe in." Sometimes it is also translated as "I am faithful." Before he became president, Abraham Lincoln had a dog named Fido.

Experts believe that the relationship between dogs and humans goes back at least 10,000 years.

Dogs have about 220 million scent receptors in their noses. Humans have between 5 and 10 million.

Activities

Activity 1: Lend a Helping Hand

Materials

Various

Directions

Plan a service project with kids. It could be as simple as writing letters to kids who are in the hospital, fund-raising for supplies for dogs in animal shelters, or making welcome kits for kids who are new to your school. You could begin by having the group brainstorm a list of causes, charities, and service opportunities that kids are interested in, and then hold a vote to choose one. Once the class has picked a cause, you could organize a fund-raiser to support it. Or, spend a day helping out. Set up a visit for your group to a local food shelf, community kitchen, animal shelter, or other organization that needs and welcomes volunteers. You could also choose to do a project that allows you to serve someone or something in your school.

Whatever service you decide to do, talk with students afterward about how it made them feel. What did they enjoy about the experience? Was performing this service different than they expected, and if so, how? What did they learn? What kind of service would they like to do next time?

Activity 2: What Makes a Hero?

Materials

None

Directions

Tell the class some stories about real dogs that showed courage and rescued people from danger. (See this website for ideas: www.dogguide.net/25-hero-dogs.php.) If you like, you could show the group pictures of the dogs you choose to talk about.

Use these dog stories as a starting point for a conversation with students about what it means to be a hero. How can we spot a hero? Is it always easy to know who might step up and be a hero in a time of need? What traits do heroes have?

Also ask kids who some of their heroes are. Invite them to write short essays or stories, talking about who their personal heroes are and why. Remind them that not all heroes are famous. Some of their biggest heroes might be in their own families or community.

Activity 3: Furry Friends

Materials
Furry Friend handout (on CD-ROM)

Directions
Make a Furry Friends display. Talk with kids about how dogs are often described as people's "best friends," and ask them to think about their own animal friends. Pass out copies of the Furry Friend handout and ask kids to draw pictures of their dogs or other pets. If they don't have pets of their own, they can depict pets belonging to friends or neighbors. Or they could imagine "dream pets" and draw pictures of these imaginary furry friends. (If you like, a few days before this activity, you could invite kids who have dogs or other pets to bring photos of them from home and attach these to their handouts.)

Next, have kids write words describing their furry friends on their handouts. Encourage them to think about more than physical characteristics and to consider ideas related to character traits. Ask kids to share what dogs or other animals have taught them about friendship, caring, or loyalty. Talk about ways that we can show these same traits to animals and to people.

When everyone has completed his or her handout, hang the pictures in your classroom or hallway.

Activity 4: Taking Care of a Pet

Materials
Pet to care for, *or* person to interview

Directions
Invite kids to spend a few days helping take care of dogs—whether their own, or those of friends or neighbors. Beforehand, talk with students about what they'll need to do. For example, they need to think about food, water, exercise, companionship, and keeping the dog and its living space clean. Afterward, have a conversation about what it was like for kids to have this responsibility. Did they enjoy it? Did they ever feel overwhelmed by the job? Were some things fun at first and not so much fun after a few days? *Note:* If some kids have allergies, ask them if there's another pet they could care for, or ask them to interview someone who cares for a dog and ask them what it's like.

Variation: If none of your students have allergies, you might get a class pet, such as a hamster, parakeet, frog, or fish. Students can take turns caring for the pet. You can talk with them about the ways that taking care of another creature helps them develop responsibility.

Lesson 11
Dolphins

Character Key Words
Helpfulness • Caring • Problem Solving • Cooperation • Respect • Conservation

Students will
- learn how dolphins behave, with each other as well as with humans, and make analogies to the ways people treat each other
- connect cooperation between dolphins and people to the idea of cooperation between people, and why it's valuable
- talk about the helpfulness that dolphins show and how it affects their relationship with people, and compare that helpfulness with human behavior
- consider the respect that many people have for dolphins, and compare that with our respect for each other, for other species, and for the environment

Overview
People have felt friendly toward dolphins for hundreds of years. From ancient Greek sailors who saw them as good luck to modern tourists and moviegoers, people have been charmed by dolphins' playfulness and their often friendly nature, along with their ability to learn skills.

Kids will be fascinated by the ways dolphins interact with people. When dolphins are respected and treated in a caring and friendly way, they appear to enjoy the company of humans. This fact can spark analogies to the ways people treat each other, and why it's important to be respectful and friendly to others. In addition, dolphins seem to help fellow animals, as well as people. They've even worked together with people to catch fish. You can use these scenarios to spark productive discussions on cooperation, problem solving, and helpfulness.

Story
Friendly Dolphins

Friendly Dolphins

In the 1900s, many ships crashed on the rocks along New Zealand's shore. Sailors had to be very careful. But they had a friend. When sailors were near the dangerous Cook Strait, they would slow down their ships and wait. Looking through spyglasses, they watched for Pelorus Jack. He was a friendly dolphin. Pelorus Jack knew these waters better than people did. He swam next to ships and guided them safely through narrow, rocky channels. Some people say that the ships Pelorus Jack guided never wrecked. Pelorus Jack grew famous. Postcards with his picture were popular.

Many other dolphins have also swum alongside ships. Dolphins probably do this to save their energy. A ship makes a wave in the water as it moves. Dolphins use this wave to help them swim faster or more easily. But for hundreds of years, sailors have considered these dolphins to be good luck.

Pelorus Jack was only one of many well-known dolphins. Everyone in New Zealand seemed to know Moko. He was a bottlenose dolphin. For years, he charmed locals and tourists. Moko seemed to enjoy playing with people at Mahia Beach. He tossed beach balls with waders. He pushed kayaks with his nose. He jumped out of the water and did flips. Local people and tourists loved Moko.

But Moko was more than a playmate. He was also a lifesaver. In 2008, a mother sperm whale and her calf got trapped near the beach. They swam into a narrow space near the shore. Then they couldn't find their way out. People tried to help the whales. But they couldn't guide them through the narrow escape route. It looked like the whales might die.

From *Building Character with True Stories from Nature* by Barbara A. Lewis, copyright © 2012. Free Spirit Publishing Inc., Minneapolis, MN; 800-735-7323; www.freespirit.com. This page may be reproduced for use within an individual classroom. For all other uses, contact www.freespirit.com/company/permissions.cfm.

Then Moko showed up. Somehow, he seemed to understand the problem. Moko made strange little grunts and whistles. The whales seemed to understand. They followed Moko to open water. The whales swam away, safe and sound.

Dolphins help each other, too. Dolphins breathe air. But sometimes when they are hurt or sick, they can't get up to the water's surface. Some dolphins have lifted others to the surface to help them get air.

The playful, helpful behavior of dolphins has made them popular with people. Dolphins have been in many movies and TV shows. They're natural stars. They even look like they're smiling!

Dolphins aren't just pretty faces, though. They are some of the smartest animals. They communicate with clicks, whistles, and grunts. They learn fast. They can be trained to understand human words and commands. They even help people do their work. In a town in Brazil, dolphins herd fish toward people waiting near shore. Then the dolphins do quick little dives in the water. This tells the fishers where to throw in their nets. The fishers respect these dolphins. They're grateful for their help. The fishers get a big catch. And the dolphins eat fish that try to swim away from the nets. Working together, the dolphins and people all get more fish than they would alone. What a team!

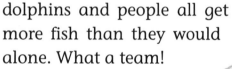

From *Building Character with True Stories from Nature* by Barbara A. Lewis, copyright © 2012. Free Spirit Publishing Inc., Minneapolis, MN; 800-735-7323; www.freespirit.com. This page may be reproduced for use within an individual classroom. For all other uses, contact www.freespirit.com/company/permissions.cfm.

Talk It Over

Use these questions to guide your students in considering analogies between dolphins and character traits and behaviors in people.

Sometimes dolphins swim next to ships. They probably do this to save energy. How can people save energy by "swimming in the same direction"? (*Note:* Kids may need a little extra help understanding this analogy. Explain that, for people, "swimming in the same direction" means working together and having a common purpose.)

- A group of people with a shared goal will reach that goal more quickly by working together.

- It can take time to agree on a shared goal and a common direction. But once you've decided on a plan, if you cooperate and focus on the same thing, you'll waste less time disagreeing.

- Whether you're on a team, doing a group project at school, or trying to get along with a sibling, working together can help everyone make a bigger difference and have more fun doing it.

Dolphins always seem like they're smiling. They aren't *really* smiling. It's just the way they look. But it helps people feel friendlier toward them. How can smiling also affect relationships that people have with each other?

- If you smile at people, they'll often smile back. Smiling helps you show that you are happy, friendly, and nice to be with.

- You meet more new people and win more friends when you smile.

- If you smile at someone, sometimes it can encourage him or her to be friendlier to you in return—even if that person doesn't know you well or hasn't been friendly to you in the past.

The people in Brazil who fish with dolphins respect their dolphin helpers. How is respect important? How can it be helpful?

- When you respect other people, they can learn to respect and trust you in return.

- People feel safer when they are around people who respect them.

- Respect can create loyalty and friendships among people.

- People will usually work harder toward a shared goal if they have respect for each other.

- When we respect animals and the environment, we work to care for them. Keeping our planet healthy is good for everyone.

Moko seemed to show problem-solving skills when he led the trapped whales to safety. Have you ever had to solve a hard problem? How did you do it? (Encourage kids to share stories about challenges they faced and overcame.)

- It can be hard to see the answer to a problem right away. We might need to "sleep on it." Sometimes the best solutions come to us when we're thinking about something else.

- Sometimes two heads are better than one. Talking to someone else about a problem can help us see the situation more clearly. The other person might have ideas about how to solve the problem.

- When we're facing a tough problem, learning more about the situation can often help us find a solution.

By helping the whales, Moko reached out to animals that were a different species from him. How do people also help others who may be different from them? Why is this important?

- Sometimes people send help, supplies, or money to faraway countries. People in those countries might be facing natural disasters or other problems.

- Sometimes people who are very different share a common goal. They may help each other and work together even though they don't agree on everything.

- Everyone needs help sometimes. It's important to care for and help others no matter what beliefs they have or what cultures they come from. Everyone deserves compassion.

Dolphin Facts

Dolphins can jump 20 feet out of the water.

Dolphins use a type of sonar called echolocation to find and track their prey, which includes fish and shrimp.

A group of dolphins is called a pod. Sometimes several pods join together in a herd.

Activities

Activity 1: To the Rescue

Materials
None

Directions
Role-play scenes in which students show someone helping or rescuing someone else. Some scenes can involve dolphins, while others may feature people only. Possible scenarios include:

- Moko rescuing the whales
- Pelorus Jack helping sailors
- rescuing someone from a fire
- helping someone who is being bullied
- dolphins helping people catch fish
- offering help to someone who is lost

Note: Some situations may be too frightening for younger kids, so choose whatever feels appropriate for your group.

After each role play, talk about what happened. How did the person doing the rescuing or helping feel? What about the kids who were being helped? If you like, extend the conversation to talk about what steps kids can take to keep themselves safe, as well as ways to help others.

Activity 2: Dolphin Stars

Materials
DVD or VHS player
TV, or projector and screen
Dolphin movie

Directions
Watch a movie about dolphins in nature. Options include the documentary IMAX film *Dolphins* (2000) or the fictional movie *Dolphin Tale* (2011). After watching the film, talk about the challenges facing dolphins in the wild. Ask kids whether they think it's important for people to respect animals and nature. What might happen if we don't treat our planet well? How can we help take care of dolphins and other wild animals?

Variation: If you live near an aquarium or zoo that has dolphins, take a field trip to see these animals in action. If possible, have a zookeeper or aquarium worker talk to the group about dolphins and their lives in the wild. Afterward, talk with kids about conservation and respect for nature and its animals.

Activity 3: Swimming in the Same Direction

Materials
Masking tape
Paper clips (1 per team)
Rulers (1 per team)
Balls (1 per team)

Preparation
This activity works best on a playground or in a large multipurpose room. Before playing the game with your group, use tape to mark out a starting line and a finish line, about 10 to 20 feet apart.

Directions

Divide your group into teams of four. (If your group doesn't divide into fours, simply make sure that each team has one object fewer than they have team members.) Ask teams to line up behind the starting line. Then hand one paper clip, ruler, and ball to the first kid in line for each team. Tell the group that the object of this game is to get all three items across the finish line. The first team to do so wins. But there's a catch: Every player on the team must carry at least one object all the way to the finish line, and no one can ever move toward the finish line without an object.

A little confusion will follow as kids figure out how best to accomplish this goal and realize that they must cooperate to make it work. For example, Team 2 is made up of Danielle, Hector, Sara, and Asad. Hector, Sara, and Asad could each carry an object to the finish line. Then Hector could return to the starting line carrying the ball and the paper clip. Finally, Danielle and Hector could each carry one of these two objects to the finish line. Or, Asad and Danielle could each carry one object, and Sara and Hector could work together to carry the third object at the same time. (For example, each of them could hold one end of the ruler.)

After the game, invite kids to describe how they figured out their plan. Did they choose team leaders? If so, how? Did they have trouble agreeing on a plan? How did they eventually make a decision? Focus on how cooperation made it easier and faster to accomplish their goal.

Lesson 12
Dragonflies

Character Key Words
Adaptability • Cooperation • Balance • Planning and Preparation • Tolerance and Acceptance

Students will
- learn about the long annual migration of dragonflies, and make analogies between this journey and good planning and preparation
- discuss the ways that working together and cooperating can make tasks easier and be more beneficial for everyone
- consider the importance of being able to adapt to new or changing situations
- think about the importance of balance in people's lives

Overview
Dragonflies work together during their life cycle and long migration, providing a strong starting point for analogies to cooperation among people to accomplish goals. Although dragonflies are not well known for their amazing migratory flight, they actually fly farther than monarch butterflies. They conserve their energy and instinctively know how to take advantage of tail winds and seasonal rainfall. Kids can make connections between the dragonfly's long migration and ideas of good planning and preparation. The dragonfly's ability to quickly change directions midair will also lead into discussions about change and adaptability. In addition, many stories and superstitions feature dragonflies. Invite your students to make analogies between these myths and the value of tolerance and acceptance.

Story
Dedicated Dragonflies

Dedicated Dragonflies

How far do you travel in a year? A mile? Hundreds of miles?

Scientists think that some kinds of dragonflies travel *very* far. Some dragonfly families travel between 9,000 and 11,000 miles in a year. They fly all the way from India to Africa—and back. This may be the longest insect migration in the world. The monarch butterfly also makes a long trip. It flies from Canada to Mexico. But the dragonfly's migration is more than three times as long as the butterfly's trek.

During their long trip, dragonflies take breaks to lay their eggs. They stop on the islands of the Maldives and the Seychelles. These tiny islands are in the Indian Ocean. Salty water surrounds them. But they don't have much fresh (nonsalty) water. Dragonflies need fresh water. They lay their eggs in it. Then young dragonflies grow up in the water. These young bugs may spend nearly five years in this water before they become adults.

So, how do dragonflies travel so far? And why do they stop at a place with so little fresh water?

The answer is in the weather. Monsoons are strong winds. They bring heavy rains with them. Dragonflies fly with the monsoons. They use the winds to help them get to the islands. Then they lay their eggs in the pools of fresh rainwater the storms leave behind. After leaving the islands, dragonflies keep gliding on the winds. They soar across the ocean to Africa. Finally, dragonflies return to India.

Dragonflies work together to make their long migration from India to Africa and back. No single dragonfly makes the full round-trip. That's because, once dragonflies leave the water and become adults, their lives are only a few weeks

From *Building Character with True Stories from Nature* by Barbara A. Lewis, copyright © 2012. Free Spirit Publishing Inc., Minneapolis, MN; 800-735-7323; www.freespirit.com. This page may be reproduced for use within an individual classroom. For all other uses, contact www.freespirit.com/company/permissions.cfm.

long. So it takes four generations of dragonflies to complete the migration. The dragonflies that go back to India are the great-grandchildren of the ones that left. No dragonfly can do it alone. But as a group, they're an unbeatable team.

The story of the dragonfly's migration is amazing and true. But many false stories and superstitions also surround dragonflies. Some are spooky. They say that dragonflies sting people or sew up their lips. Other stories describe them as fairies or spirits.

Some dragonfly tales are more cheerful. In Japan, dragonflies are good luck. In Denmark, a dragonfly is a sign that wealth is on its way. Some people in England make wishes when they see these bugs.

Why do people tell all these stories about dragonflies? That's hard to know. Maybe it's because of their big eyes. Maybe their shimmery wings make them look like fairies. Or maybe dragonflies' rapid, acrobatic flying just leaves people in awe. Dragonflies have four wings, and they control each wing separately. This makes them quick and nimble. Dragonflies can stop midair and change direction in a moment. They zigzag through the sky at up to 35 miles per hour. These use this fancy flying to catch their meals.

Dragonflies are good bugs to have around, because they eat other bugs that can be pests, like mosquitoes and flies. Most slower-moving bugs can't get away from the zooming dragons. And the dragonflies eat a *lot*. A single dragonfly can eat its own weight in bugs in thirty minutes. So if you're worried about mosquitoes or flies at your next picnic, maybe you should invite a few dragonflies!

From *Building Character with True Stories from Nature* by Barbara A. Lewis, copyright © 2012. Free Spirit Publishing Inc., Minneapolis, MN; 800-735-7323; www.freespirit.com. This page may be reproduced for use within an individual classroom. For all other uses, contact www.freespirit.com/company/permissions.cfm.

Talk It Over

Use these questions to guide your students in considering analogies between dragonflies and cooperation, preparation, and other character traits and behaviors in people.

When dragonflies migrate, they save energy by using monsoons to help them travel farther. They also work together to complete the full round-trip. How can working together help people?

- When people work together on their goals, they create good plans and participate in making good decisions. That organization helps them achieve more.

- When people face problems they can't solve, they look for new solutions. Most famous inventors ran into lots of problems before they succeeded. For example, Thomas Edison tried hundreds of ways to make the lightbulb before he found something that worked. He kept trying.

People tell many myths about dragonflies. But dragonflies don't *really* sew up people's mouths, they don't bite or sting people, and they are not fairies. Why do you think people enjoy telling stories, even when they're untrue? How can this be harmful? Can it ever be helpful?

- Sometimes people can make up problems that aren't really there. They can worry over things that aren't really a big deal. This can make them feel unhappy and stressed.

- When people don't know how something works, sometimes they make up stories to explain it.

- If we tell untrue or unkind stories about other people, we can hurt their feelings or damage their reputations. We can also get in trouble for making up things.

- Telling stories can be creative and fun. It can help us think about things in new and different ways.

- Sometimes a story inspires you to learn more about a topic. Then you might learn something that will help you in the future.

Dragonflies can stop midair and change directions very quickly. Can you compare this with people who change directions?

- People can get into ruts when they do things the same way every time. Sometimes this feels comfortable and safe. But change is good, too. It helps us be creative and stay interested in what we're doing.

- Sometimes we need to be able to stop and look for a new solution if what we're doing isn't working well. We might have to stop right in the middle of a project to rethink our plan and change directions. This can be hard, but it's usually better than continuing to go in a direction that isn't working.

- Always keep your mind open to new ideas and be willing to change your direction or reverse.

Nature's food web keeps its creatures in balance. For example, dragonflies eat mosquitoes. And birds eat dragonflies. When the food web gets off-balance, the world ends up with too many or too few of some animals. Can you think of any way that this idea relates to people's lives?

- It's important to keep the different parts of your life in balance. These different parts might include schoolwork, chores, play, friendships, family, good nutrition, exercise, clubs, teams, a faith community, service, Internet activity, and so on.

- You can help keep your life balanced by making sure to take time for the different things your mind and body need.

- When we have a lot to do, it can be hard to keep everything straight. It helps to make to-do lists so that we don't forget anything.

- Everyone feels out of balance sometimes. This is normal. Some weeks you might have tons of homework, and other weeks you might hang out with friends a whole lot. It's okay if some things get unbalanced once in a while. But if you feel this way a lot of the time, it can be stressful. You may need to figure out how to make changes so that you feel calmer and more balanced.

Dragonflies spend most of their lives preparing to become adult dragonflies and to make their long, long journey. What are some similar situations in people's lives?

- Sometimes you may have to work for a long time before you get what you want or need. For example, you might work hard and go to school for many years because you want to have a certain kind of job when you grow up.

- When you have a big goal, getting there can be part of the fun. Make sure your journey is a great one.

Dragonfly Facts

Dragonflies catch their insect prey by grabbing it with their feet.

Dragonflies can fly straight up and down, and can hover in midair like tiny helicopters.

Fossils show that prehistoric ancestors of the dragonfly had wingspans of more than 2 feet.

Activities

Activity 1: Dragonfly Directions

Materials
Dragonfly Directions handout (on CD-ROM)
Optional: Pencils, markers, and crayons

Directions
Pass out copies of the Dragonfly Directions handout showing the dragonfly's migratory route. If desired, invite kids to color the map, draw dragonflies along the route, or decorate the handout in other ways. Talk with kids about what they see on the map. What do they notice about the islands where dragonflies stop? (*Examples:* They're very small. They're far apart.) Compare the dragonfly's long journey and its pre-planned stops to the way people need to know where they're going. Discuss literal interpretations of this, such as kids staying safe when walking to friends' homes, or making sure to always tell adults where they're going. Also remind kids that not all destinations are physical. A goal—whether it's getting a good grade, winning at a sports event, or giving a musical performance—is also a destination.

You might also talk about the way dragonflies can change directions when they're hunting other bugs. Are detours ever helpful in people's lives? Is there a way to be open to new ideas and new perspectives without losing focus on the big goal?

Activity 2: Taking a Trip

Materials
Taking a Trip handout (on CD-ROM)

Directions
Pass out copies of the Taking a Trip handout. Invite kids to imagine that they're taking a big journey. Encourage them to get creative with their ideas. Maybe their trip will take them to the Great Wall of China, to the moon, or into the past. Wherever they're going, they need to plan for their journey. Have kids think about what they need to pack. (*For example:* Chinese dictionary, spacesuit, map of ancient Rome.) Also advise them to think about what they need to do before they leave. (*For example:* Get a passport, make sure someone's feeding the goldfish, study local customs of their destination.) Kids can brainstorm on notebook paper first, and then, when they're happy with their lists, they can fill in the spaces on the handout.

As students work, talk about why planning is a good idea. Ask them what they think might happen if they don't plan carefully enough, or if they forget something really important. Remind them that this kind of preparation is also helpful when it comes to doing a big project. Being organized and prepared can make things a lot easier down the road.

Activity 3: Balancing Act

Materials

Skirt/pant hanger (with 2 clips at the bottom)
Objects to "weigh" (for example, pencils, pieces of paper, small pieces of wood or cloth)

Preparation

Before beginning this activity with your students, gather several objects to "weigh," making sure that each of them can be held up by the hanger's clips. Suspend the hanger from a solid, straight support in your classroom and make sure that it hangs evenly. If it tilts to one side, adjust the clips by sliding them away from or toward the center of the hanger, or attach a very small weight to one end so that the hanger is balanced.

Directions

To begin the activity, show kids the even, balanced "scale." Talk about the way this represents a balanced life, in which many different parts are working in harmony.

Then add a weight to one side. As the hanger tilts to that side, talk with kids about how the scale now represents a life that has gotten out of balance. Ask them to name things that might throw off *their* balance. For example, some students might have trouble getting their homework done because they're involved in so many activities. Others might get so stressed about schoolwork that they forget to have enough fun. Talk about what each of us can do to keep ourselves in balance.

As you discuss these ideas, you can also continue to experiment with hanging different objects from each clip. Show that it can take time to find the right balance.

Lesson 13
Elephants

Character Key Words
Friendship • Caring • Tolerance and Acceptance • Peacefulness • Respect

Students will
- learn about elephants and their relationships with each other, as well as their relationship to humans
- think about the unusual friendship between Tarra the elephant and Bella the dog, and make analogies to friendships among people
- make comparisons between elephants burying their dead to people mourning losses
- consider the aggression shown by some elephants and make an analogy to people who show angry or hostile behavior
- compare the behavior of orphaned elephants to the way people without positive role models might act

Overview
Elephants are sometimes said to never forget. And in fact, they do have long memories. They have recognized each other even after years of separation. Many scientists place them among the most intelligent animals on the planet. In addition, they form firm and sometimes unexpected friendships. Kids will draw natural connections between elephant friendships and behaviors of caring, trust, and open-mindedness among people.

There is also a darker side to elephant behavior, however. The number of elephant attacks on people has increased over the years, and experts have multiple theories for this pattern, which is sometimes called the Human-Elephant Conflict. One theory is that orphaned young elephants lack good adult role models. When comparing this to situations in people's lives, your students can think about how violent behavior may be learned—and, similarly, how good character traits can also be taught by example and by observation.

Story
Amazing Elephants

Amazing Elephants

"Elephants never forget."

Have you heard this saying? Really, elephants probably forget lots of things. But they *do* seem to have long memories.

For example, when an elephant dies, other elephants bury the body. They use dirt and sticks to cover it. Then they come back to visit the bones for years.

Here's another example of elephant memory.

Jenny and Shirley were two elephants that had worked together at a circus. Then they were apart for more than twenty years. But when they both ended up at a home for retired elephants in Tennessee, they got excited. Jenny reached out to Shirley with her trunk. The two elephants seemed to know each other. Jenny and Shirley remembered each other. And once they were together again, they wanted to stay that way. They hardly ever spent time apart.

Many elephants seem to form close friendships. Sometimes these friendships are unusual. Tarra is another elephant at the Tennessee home. Her best buddy was a dog named Bella.

Tarra and Bella explored the woods. They played in fields and splashed in ponds. They ran through the snow in the winter, and enjoyed the warm sun in the summer. Tarra's big gray body is over 8 feet tall. She weighs almost 9,000 pounds. Bella was a small yellow dog with big brown eyes. Bella and Tarra didn't seem to care that they were so different. They just liked being together.

Elephants have also reached and helped animals. For example, a group of elephants in South Africa came to the rescue of antelopes. People had captured the antelopes and locked them up in a fenced-in

From *Building Character with True Stories from Nature* by Barbara A. Lewis, copyright © 2012. Free Spirit Publishing Inc., Minneapolis, MN; 800-735-7323; www.freespirit.com. This page may be reproduced for use within an individual classroom. For all other uses, contact www.freespirit.com/company/permissions.cfm.

area. Eleven elephants quietly circled the fence. Then the elephants' female leader walked up to the gate. She unlocked the metal latches with her trunk and swung the gate open. After the antelopes escaped into the night, the elephants left, too. They didn't even stay to snack on the antelopes' food.

But elephants aren't always friendly or helpful. Sometimes they charge into villages. They can wreck homes. They have hurt and killed people. Elephants are huge. And they can run as fast as 30 miles per hour. You don't want to be in an angry elephant's way.

But *why* are they angry? Why are they attacking people?

Some people call this the Human-Elephant Conflict, or HEC. About 500 people die in elephant attacks each year. But the HEC isn't one-sided. People kill about 1,000 elephants every year. Humans are adult elephants' only natural predators. People kill elephants for their ivory tusks, to protect homes and crops, and out of fear.

It hasn't always been this way. Elephants have been helpers to people for years. So what changed?

Some elephant experts think it's a space problem. Elephants used to live in places with few people. But now elephants and many people are sharing space. Maybe elephants need more room. They could be trying to protect their homes.

Experts also have another idea. Elephant tusks are very valuable. Hunters have killed many adult elephants for their tusks. This can leave elephant babies without mothers to teach them how to behave. Without guides, some young elephants form teenage mobs. They get into trouble. Groups of young males roam around the countryside. They attack cars and trample crops. They charge at people and animals with their heavy hooves and sharp tusks.

But wildlife workers figured something out. They sent some of these troublemakers to live with older elephants. The older elephants didn't put up with tantrums from the younger elephants. They taught them how to act. Soon, the young elephants' behavior improved. Maybe even elephants need someone to teach them good manners.

From *Building Character with True Stories from Nature* by Barbara A. Lewis, copyright © 2012. Free Spirit Publishing Inc., Minneapolis, MN; 800-735-7323; www.freespirit.com. This page may be reproduced for use within an individual classroom. For all other uses, contact www.freespirit.com/company/permissions.cfm.

Talk It Over

Use these questions to guide your students in considering analogies between elephants and respect, friendship, and other character traits and behaviors in people.

Elephants seem to have rituals related to death and mourning. How is this similar to people?

- People have rituals to mourn people who die. These rituals vary from culture to culture. But all of these different traditions are important and valuable.

- It's important to take the time to mourn a loss in some way. It helps us start to heal and feel better.

Elephants appear to have good memories. Some have even recognized each other after twenty years apart. How can you compare this to human behavior?

- Strong friendships can last for a lifetime. Sometimes close friends still feel connected even after not seeing each other for a long time.

- Both good memories and bad memories can stay with people for a long time. It's natural for people who survive dangerous or scary events such as hurricanes or wars to continue to feel sad and afraid long after these experiences. Happy memories can also last a long time. Sometimes if you're feeling sad, it helps to think about a cheerful memory.

Tarra and Bella were very different in appearance, but they were good friends. Can you think of ways this is similar to friendships between people?

- Even people who seem very different on the surface can become close friends.

- When you get to know someone better, you may learn that you are more alike than you are different.

- True friends don't care what you look like. They care about you because of who you are on the inside.

Even though elephants are usually friendly and gentle, sometimes they attack people. Can you make an analogy between this idea and being careful in situations or activities that might become dangerous?

- Places that look safe may not be. If you go someplace new, be aware of your surroundings.

- Even if you are a good swimmer, you should not swim alone. You might get hurt and not have anyone there to help.

- Be careful about what you eat and drink. Things that might be okay in small amounts can be unhealthful if we eat or drink too much of them. And harmful substances such as drugs are never safe to take, even in tiny amounts.

Elephants seem to be peaceful most of the time, but elephant attacks are on the rise. Some experts think that the Human-Elephant Conflict is happening because elephants and people are sharing space. Do people ever argue or fight about space? What are some examples?

- Family members need to have certain space for themselves. Sometimes people need to be alone for a while to think or just to relax.

- Neighbors may disagree or argue about shared space, boundaries, or noise.

- Sometimes countries try to take control of the land and resources of other countries. This can lead to war.

Some young elephants that lose their mothers become aggressive. But when they live with adult elephants, their behavior improves. Can you compare this to human behavior?

- Kids whose parents or other role models don't model positive traits might show negative behaviors.

- We all need people to look up to, no matter how old we are.

- Kids who gain good role models can change their behavior and can learn positive character traits.

- *Note:* If desired, you can share this information with students and talk about it with them: Some experts think that some elephants are aggressive because they have seen other elephants being attacked or killed. Similarly, research suggests that people who see regular acts of violence can become more aggressive. According to a study by the American Academy of Child & Adolescent Psychiatry, kids and teens who often see violent acts on TV may grow numb to violence and even imitate it.

Elephant Facts

Elephants live in hot parts of the world. An elephant's big ears radiate heat from the body to help keep the animal cool.

Elephants are the world's largest land animals. African elephants are slightly larger than Asian elephants.

An elephant trunk contains about 100,000 muscles.

Activities

Activity 1: The Kindness Project

Materials
Slips of paper
Box or other container

Directions
Invite each kid to make a secret plan to do something nice for someone he or she knows. If you choose to keep this activity inside the classroom, write each student's name on a slip of paper and put these slips in a box or other container. Then have kids draw one name each from the box, ensuring that all kids are included.

Alternatively, you could have kids choose to show kindness to people outside of your classroom. If you take this route, ask kids to try to choose people who are not already their close friends. For example, a student might select a different teacher, a new kid in a club, or a neighbor.

Suggest that kids do three nice things over the course of a week for the person they've chosen. For example, someone might make a special effort to include someone in games; write a nice anonymous note to him or her; or ask about his or her day. Encourage kids to pay attention to how people respond to their kind actions.

After the week is over, talk with kids about how the kindness project went. How did they feel when they did these nice things? Did they want to tell the people about what they were doing, or did they enjoy keeping it a secret? How did the people respond? Did they seem friendlier, happier, or more peaceful? Did kids notice the people acting more kindly to other people in turn?

Activity 2: Words of Friendship

Materials
Index cards or pieces of construction paper (4 to 6 per student)
Markers or crayons

Directions
Hand out index cards or paper and markers or crayons. Invite kids to write down several words—one on each card—to describe their friends, without using names. Ask them not to use any words describing their friends' physical characteristics. Suggest a few words to get them started, such as *funny, thoughtful,* and *artistic*. Gather the cards, mix them up, and choose a random one out of the bunch. Read the word aloud and ask kids to talk about why this quality is good to have in a friend. (Don't ask kids to identify themselves as the writers.) If there are any negative

qualities listed, address them honestly. Discuss the fact that everyone has flaws, and that we love our friends despite their flaws. In turn, good friends do the same for us.

Activity 3: Act and React

Materials

8-inch balloon
Optional: Roller skates or in-line skates
Optional: Ball

Directions

Demonstrate Newton's Third Law of Motion: For every action, there is an equal and opposite reaction. Use this principle to show kids how acts of kindness or unkindness have an effect on the people around them.

Inflate the balloon but don't tie off the end. Then let go of the balloon and watch it shoot around the room. Explain that the *action* was forcing air into the balloon. The *reaction* was the air quickly leaving the balloon.

Variation: If you have a student who is comfortable and competent on roller skates or in-line skates, ask him or her to put them on and stand at the front of the room holding the ball. Ask him or her to toss the ball to you. What happens? (As the student throws the ball forward, he or she will roll backward.)

Talk with kids about how these actions and reactions are similar to the way unkind or violent actions can sometimes cause unkind or violent reactions. Compare it also to acts of kindness encouraging acts of kindness in return. Discuss ways that we can be careful that our actions result in positive reactions rather than negative ones.

Activity 4: Imagine That

Materials

Journals

Directions

Ask students to write about what would happen if children were raised by robots, computers, or other kids, rather than by their parents. Would that be fun? Exciting? Scary? Lonely? What would the world be like? How might kids' behavior and actions change? Do we need real people to show us how to behave and how to care for each other? Or could machines do the job? Encourage kids to let their imaginations roam.

Give kids twenty minutes or so to write, and then discuss their ideas as a group. Talk about the many ways that parents, teachers, and other grown-ups help care for and take care of kids. Also talk about the way kids help and care for each other, and even for grown-ups.

Lesson 14
Fireflies

Character Key Words
Honesty • Integrity • Good Decision-Making

Students will
- learn interesting facts about fireflies, such as the purposes of their flashing lights
- compare the male fireflies that get tricked and eaten to people who make poor choices and can't predict or control the consequences
- compare and contrast the behavior of some fireflies that trick their predators and their prey with people of integrity who are true to what they say
- make analogies between fireflies' energy-efficient light and people who save their energy in various ways

Overview
If your students live in an area where fireflies are common, you will have special fun with this story. Many of them will have chased fireflies and captured them in bottles. However, they might not have wondered how fireflies make their light, or why. They will be intrigued by the answers.

You can compare the firefly's special talent of creating light—and its various ways of using that light—to human behaviors that involve integrity and honesty. This lesson can also help students consider the value of thinking carefully and using good judgment when making decisions. They can learn that they are free to make choices, but that they can't always know or control the consequences of those choices.

Story
Flickering Fireflies

Flickering Fireflies

It's a warm summer night. It's almost time to go inside. But you're having so much fun. Just five more minutes . . .

Wait. What's that?

A light flashes. You see a glowing, greenish-yellow dot. It darts across the grass—and disappears. You spin around searching for it. Then you spot the light again, and again. Suddenly, dozens of lights are dancing in the dark. What are they?

These flickering lights are fireflies. Sometimes they are called lightning bugs. Have you ever caught one in a jar and watched it flash?

People have loved the firefly's beautiful glow for hundreds of years. These bugs like to live where it's warm. They especially like damp, humid places. They flutter around ponds, marshes, and trees. They flicker and flash in long grass.

Fireflies use their light to attract mates. A flashing male will fly toward a female firefly. If she's interested, she returns the flash. They flash back and forth to communicate. There are about 2,000 different kinds of fireflies. Each type has its own flash pattern. This special pattern is like a secret language. It helps fireflies find the right mates.

But some female fireflies play a trick. They copy the flashes of other lightning bugs. This can fool a male firefly. He thinks he sees a friend. But when the confused male firefly lands near the female, she pounces on him and eats him for dinner.

From *Building Character with True Stories from Nature* by Barbara A. Lewis, copyright © 2012. Free Spirit Publishing Inc., Minneapolis, MN; 800-735-7323; www.freespirit.com. This page may be reproduced for use within an individual classroom. For all other uses, contact www.freespirit.com/company/permissions.cfm.

The firefly's flashes can also send a warning. The warning says, "Don't eat me! I don't taste good." And to most animals, fireflies definitely don't taste good. In fact, some fireflies are poisonous.

How do fireflies make their special light? Chemicals inside the firefly's body create its glow. A firefly's light can be yellow, green, or pale red. Even baby fireflies make light. These young fireflies are called glowworms.

Fireflies may look a bit like tiny lamps, but they have a special skill. When you turn on a lamp, the bulb gets warm. Most lightbulbs lose 90 percent of their energy on heat. That's a big waste of energy. If a firefly heated up like a lightbulb, it would burn itself up. Poof! But the firefly wastes almost no energy on heat. Almost all of its energy turns into light.

Imagine how much energy we could save if we used firefly light in our homes, schools, and shops. Saving energy is good for the earth and the environment. We can't *really* light the world with fireflies. But scientists are trying to learn how fireflies make cold light. Maybe someday they will discover it. The firefly's secret could light up the dark and save energy, too.

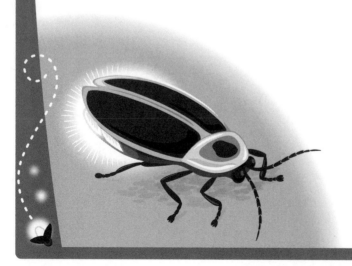

From *Building Character with True Stories from Nature* by Barbara A. Lewis, copyright © 2012. Free Spirit Publishing Inc., Minneapolis, MN; 800-735-7323; www.freespirit.com. This page may be reproduced for use within an individual classroom. For all other uses, contact www.freespirit.com/company/permissions.cfm.

Talk It Over

Use these questions to guide your students in considering analogies between fireflies and integrity, good judgment, and other character traits and behaviors in people.

Fireflies use their light to attract mates and as a warning signal to predators. Some fireflies also use their light to trick prey into coming close. Can you make a comparison with people who use lies or deception to gain something?

- People sometimes make false promises because they want to gain popularity, power, or admiration.

- Sometimes people cheat on tests or homework because they want good grades but don't want to do the work.

- People may lie about themselves and their lives because they want to impress others.

Sometimes fireflies get tricked into making poor choices and landing near other fireflies that eat them. It's not always easy to tell when a choice will have serious results. What can people do to protect themselves from making dangerous choices?

- When you feel scared or worried, talk to someone you trust. Usually making the right choice feels good inside, even if it's a difficult decision.

- Make a list of good and bad things that might happen as the result of a choice. Ask yourself if your choice will harm or help you or others. Use this information to make the best choice.

- Avoid making choices that cause you to lie, or that conflict with your beliefs. Always try to stay true to your inner self.

- Remember that everyone makes poor decisions sometimes. That doesn't make them bad people. You can always learn from a bad choice and make a better decision the next time.

Lightbulbs lose a lot of energy when they are on. But fireflies have the amazing ability to make light without losing much energy in the form of heat. **What are some ways that people can save their energy and use it wisely?**

- When you have a problem, you can save energy if you can talk about your problem calmly instead of getting upset.

- If you get good sleep at night, you will be able to work and play better during the day.

- If you tell the truth, you won't have to waste energy making up lies and trying to remember them.

- If you get your homework, chores, or other duties done on time, you won't waste energy being frustrated when you fall behind.

- Do your most important jobs first. It's easy and tempting to get sidetracked playing games, watching TV, or hanging out with friends. But then you might run out of time or get too tired to do the jobs you need to do.

Firefly Facts

Fireflies produce their light using cells near their abdomens. This natural light is called bioluminescence.

Some adult fireflies feed on pollen and nectar. Others do not eat at all during their short lives.

Scientists have used the firefly enzyme luciferase and its glowing properties to find blood clots and certain kinds of cells.

Activities

Activity 1: Firefly Poems

Materials

Firefly Poem handouts (on the CD-ROM)

Directions

Hand out copies of the Firefly Poem handouts. Depending on your group's ages, interests, and abilities, you may choose not to use all of the different handouts. Distribute roughly equal numbers of each handout that you choose. Invite kids to fill in the forms with acrostic poems about fireflies, and ask them to focus on character traits and behaviors. If kids aren't familiar with acrostic poems, model one on the board to show them how they work. For example:

Caring

Happy

Open

Integrity

Character

Example

If desired, younger kids can work in small groups, or the class can compose poems together as a big group.

When students have written their poems, invite kids to share them if they feel comfortable doing so. Talk about the poems as a group. Did they cause anyone to think about fireflies and character in new ways? What did kids find fun about writing the poems? What was challenging? How did people's ideas differ?

Activity 2: The Good Decisions Toolbox

Materials

None

Directions

Talk with kids about specific ways they can make positive choices. Brainstorm a list of ideas and write them on the board. For example:

- Take time to think about a decision carefully.

- Ask the advice of someone you respect.

- Learn all you can about your choice before making it.

- Think about whether you would feel comfortable sharing your choice with your mom or dad, best friend, older sister or brother, coach, or teacher.

- Brainstorm the possible results—positive and negative—of your choice.

- Listen to the voice inside you. If you have to talk yourself into it, and it doesn't feel right, it probably isn't.

- Get a good night's sleep before making your choice.

Discuss each idea and how it might be helpful. Also consider the ways it might be hard to follow these suggestions at times.

When you have a list that the group is happy with, make copies of the list and hand them out, or ask kids to copy the list into their notebooks. Tell them that this list is like a toolbox. When they have big decisions to make, they can use these tools to help them succeed. Remind kids that making one positive choice makes it easier to make another. Over time, they can make a habit of good judgment and decision-making.

Activity 3: Character Speeches

Materials

Slips of paper with scenarios written on them
Box, hat, or other container

Preparation

Write short character situations on slips of paper, fold them in half, and put them in a box or other container.

Example character situations:

- You are at the checkout counter at a store, and the salesperson gives you back too much change. What should you do and say?

- You have a friend who is telling lies about you, and you are afraid people will believe those lies. What should you do?

- You see a student taking money from another kid's desk at school. You don't want to be a tattler, but you also want to be honest. What will you do?

- You choose to go to a party. At the party, the kids start watching a violent movie. You want these kids to be your friends, but you know it's not a good choice for you to watch the movie. What could you do?

- Your mom tells you to be home at a certain time. But you're having so much fun with your friend that you get home late. Luckily, your mom isn't home yet either. She won't know that you were late. What should you do?

- You didn't do your homework that was due today. You lie to your teacher and tell her you lost it, and she gives you one extra day to hand it in. But you really don't want to do it. So you copy your friend's paper and hand it in. Your teacher notices that your homework is identical and asks to talk to both you and your friend. One of the class rules is that if you cheat, you get a failing grade. What should you do?

- You find out that your big brother is taking drugs. You're worried about him. But he says you'll be in big trouble if you tell anyone. What should you do?

Directions

Have students give spontaneous speeches about honesty and integrity. Allow two or three students to each draw one slip of paper from the box. Ask kids to read the character situations on their slips to themselves first. Then give them about five minutes or so to think of something to say about the situations they've drawn. Explain that spontaneous speeches don't need to be long (especially if you're working with younger kids), but that they should be more than a sentence or two. If desired, you can model an example of a short speech yourself.

You can do this activity periodically, doing only one or two speeches at a time. It will help kids develop their speaking ability as well as encourage them to think about positive character traits.

Lesson 15
Horses

Character Key Words
Service • Perseverance • Loyalty • Responsibility • Cooperation

Students will
- learn interesting facts about horses, including their important role in human history
- consider the ways horses show dedication, responsibility, and loyalty, and make connections between those characteristics and human behavior
- make analogies between the hard work and cooperation that horses show and the service that people do for others

Overview
Horses have carried many famous soldiers into battle. They have also held starring roles in many movies and books. In fact, their contribution to human history may be the most important of any animal. Horses have served people in many ways, from building roads to harvesting crops to saving the lives of their riders. They have also carried people on their strong backs, helping spread cultures and share new ideas. It might even be said that history has been built on the backs of horses. And these faithful animals have shown great perseverance and dedication. All of these traits will provide a good starting point for having a conversation with your students about analogous traits and behaviors in people.

Story
Heroic Horses

Heroic Horses

Maybe you've heard that dogs are people's best friends. Dogs *are* great friends. But sometimes people say that history has been written on the backs of horses. Thousands of years ago, people learned that horses are good workers. They are strong and loyal. Horses have pulled carts, carried food, and worked on farms. They have helped build roads. They have even pulled trains.

People also learned to ride horses. On horseback, people could travel faster and farther. This helped spread and share ideas between different countries and cultures.

Soldiers found that horses were helpful in battle, too. They are fast learners and follow directions well. Many warhorses grew famous. For example, Bucephalus was Alexander the Great's favorite horse. Alexander was a ruler from ancient Greece. Bucephalus helped him win many battles. When the horse died, Alexander built a city in his honor. The Spanish fighter El Cid also trusted his horse, which was named Babieca. The French leader Napoleon rode his horse Marengo into battle many times. The list goes on and on.

One famous American warhorse was named Comanche. He carried an army captain in the Battle of the Little Bighorn. This battle was in 1876. It was between the U.S. Army and a group of Native Americans. The army lost badly. Comanche's rider died. So did many other soldiers, and most of the army's horses. After the battle ended, soldiers found Comanche. He had been lying on the battlefield for two days. He was badly hurt. Because Comanche had been so loyal and brave, people took good care of him. The rest of his life was calm and peaceful. When he died, he was honored with a military funeral.

Horses have also been sports stars. Famous racehorses include Haleb, Seabiscuit, and War Admiral. They surprised everyone with their determination. They set new records for speed. Horses have even starred in TV shows and movies. Or maybe you'd rather read

From *Building Character with True Stories from Nature* by Barbara A. Lewis, copyright © 2012. Free Spirit Publishing Inc., Minneapolis, MN; 800-735-7323; www.freespirit.com. This page may be reproduced for use within an individual classroom. For all other uses, contact www.freespirit.com/company/permissions.cfm.

about horses. If so, you're in luck! There are thousands of books about horses.

Many other horses are not famous. But that doesn't matter to their human friends. What really matters is the love and respect that people feel for their horses. Sometimes people even owe their lives to horses. For example, an English farmer named Fiona has a story about a heroic horse. Fiona was out in a field trying to help a young cow. All of a sudden, the cow's protective mother knocked Fiona down. Then the mother cow sat right on top of Fiona! That may sound funny, but it's no laughing matter. Cows can weigh 1,000 pounds or more. Fiona couldn't move. She could hardly breathe. She was afraid she might die. But then Fiona's horse, Kerry, raced to her rescue. Kerry kicked the cow with its hooves. Finally the cow stood up. Fiona was hurt, but she was safe.

Another horse lover tells of a very scary ride. A young girl was riding her horse. Suddenly, a coyote jumped in their path. He attacked the horse and nipped at its heels. The girl fell to the ground. She was afraid the coyote would hurt her. But her loyal horse kicked the coyote away over and over. The coyote finally gave up. Then the girl's horse carried her home. The horse may have saved her life.

Horses also help people who face health challenges. Horses can be patient and gentle. Scientists think that just being near horses changes how the human brain works. Horses can make us feel calmer. Some people learn to communicate better after spending time with these special animals.

So from helping build roads to helping us feel better, horses can make us happier and healthier.

From *Building Character with True Stories from Nature* by Barbara A. Lewis, copyright © 2012. Free Spirit Publishing Inc., Minneapolis, MN; 800-735-7323; www.freespirit.com. This page may be reproduced for use within an individual classroom. For all other uses, contact www.freespirit.com/company/permissions.cfm.

Talk It Over

Use these questions to guide your students in considering analogies between horses and responsibility, service, and other character traits and behaviors in people.

Horses have been good helpers to people for many years, partly because they are good at following orders. Can you make a connection between this and human behavior?

- People who receive orders and work hard don't always get a lot of glory or recognition. But hard work and dedication are very important. No big project could happen without them.

- If everyone tried to give orders, it would lead to confusion and chaos. We all need to learn to cooperate to get a job done.

- The brain tells the body what to do, but the arms, hands, legs, and feet carry out the work.

- If you are willing to listen to suggestions, you can learn new ways of doing things.

Comanche's story shows that sometimes respect and honor can come even when we fail to reach a goal. Can you relate this idea to people who don't succeed but keep trying?

- Sometimes not succeeding at something the first time makes us try harder the next time.

- You can learn a lot about patience, hard work, dedication, and courage if you persevere even when you face big challenges.

- The only real failure is giving up or quitting. Continuing to try, even when it's hard, is something to be proud of.

Many dedicated horses have protected their riders and stayed faithful to them even in dangerous situations. Can you think of things that people dedicate themselves to? How can this be good? Can it ever be bad?

- When we are dedicated to people, groups, or ideas, we are likely to work hard for them.

- Dedicating yourself to positive character traits such as honesty, caring, responsibility, and respect can help you make good decisions and stay safe when you are in confusing or dangerous situations. It can also help you protect others.

- Sometimes we feel dedicated to friends who have negative behaviors. This can be confusing. When those friends or those behaviors start to make us feel uncomfortable, it's a good idea to talk to someone we trust about what to do.

Horses have a calming effect on some people. Can you see a relationship between this and human behavior?

- People who are patient and caring can help other people feel calm. When people are calm, they can think more clearly and make better decisions.

- Gentle people often make others feel comfortable and safe.

- Sometimes just listening to someone else when he or she is upset or sad can be a big help.

Horse Facts

Historians think that nomads living on the Asian steppe first domesticated horses about 4,000 years ago.

An ancient ancestor of the horse, called the Sifrhippus sandrae, weighed only about 8.5 to 15 pounds. It lived in North America about 56 million years ago.

A newborn horse, called a foal, can stand up within about one hour of being born.

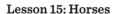

Activities

Activity 1: Growing and Changing

Materials

Growing and Changing handout (on CD-ROM)

Directions

The contributions and responsibilities of horses have changed over time. A person's activities and responsibilities also change during his or her life. Kids will enjoy thinking about what they used to do (and not do) as babies and toddlers, and imagining what they might do in the future. As they consider these ideas, you can guide them to think about the bigger ideas of caring for others and having new and changing responsibilities.

Pass out copies of the Growing and Changing handout and have kids fill it out individually, or project the handout on a screen or board and complete it as a group. For example, in the "When I was a baby" section, kids might answer, "I drank milk" or "I slept a lot." As you move through the other sections of the handout, remind kids to think about what other people have done and will do for them at each period in their lives, and also what they can do for themselves and for others.

Encourage kids to think about how they can contribute more and care for others more as they get older. What are the benefits and drawbacks of each stage in their lives? Do they miss anything about being younger? What are they most excited about as they grow older? How can responsibility be rewarding? Is it ever scary or difficult? Discuss their answers as a group.

Activity 2: Cooperative Catch

Materials

Blankets or pieces of cloth about 3 or 4 feet across
    (1 per team)
Foam balls (1 per team)

Directions

Note: This activity works best on a playground or in a large multipurpose room.

Divide kids into groups of four. Have each member of each team hold one corner of the team's blanket, holding it flat and parallel to the floor. Place a ball in the center of each team's blanket. Tell kids that they need to use the blanket to toss the ball up into the air and to catch it again with the blanket. The team that successfully catches the ball the most times in five minutes wins.

After playing, discuss the importance of cooperation and working together as a team. What happened if kids worked against each other? Horses that work in teams are more successful than ones that fight against their harnesses. People who work cooperatively in teams will also be more successful in what they do. Plus, the work will probably be more fun.

Activity 3: "I Think I Can"

Materials

Story of perseverance (such as *The Little Engine That Could, The Tortoise and the Hare,* or another of your choice)

Directions

Read the story about perseverance aloud to the class. Discuss what kept the main character trying during the story. How would the story have been different if the character had given up? Talk about the idea of perseverance, and make sure that kids understand what it means. You might also remind kids of how much horses have accomplished throughout history through their perseverance. Ask kids to think about perseverance in their own lives. When have they been in situations that required them to keep trying even when it was very difficult? How did they handle these challenges?

Next, ask each student to make two lists. The first list is of things that are hard for him or her to do. The second list is of things the student finds pretty easy to do. Discuss why some things are harder than others. Talk with kids about how everyone has different talents, and how this makes the world a fun and interesting place. Also discuss how, if you practice a skill long enough and if you have patience, you will improve at it. Invite kids to share examples of skills or talents that they have already practiced and gotten better at, as well as ones they still want to work on. Ask why these things interest them. Explore the rewards of perseverance. How does it feel to reach a goal after working hard? What can we do to keep motivating ourselves even when things get tough?

Lesson 16
Metalmark Moths

Character Key Words
Courage • Integrity • Good Decision-Making • Fairness and Equality

Students will
- learn about the metalmark moth's ability to mimic the jumping spider, its main predator
- make analogies between the metalmark moth's mimicking and the way people sometimes copy others
- compare the metalmark moth's bold faceoff with the jumping spider to the courage shown by a person who stands up to someone who bullies others
- talk about what it means to stand up for what you believe, and what the positive and negative results can be

Overview
Metalmark moths mimic the appearance and behavior of the jumping spiders that prey on them. For a moment, this mimicry confuses the spider. Most of the time, this gives the moth time to escape safely. The moth's bold behavior provides an opportunity for you and your students to make analogies to integrity, courage, and standing up for what you believe.

The metalmark moth story also provides a good jumping-off point for discussing the ways that mimicking poor behavior can lead to poor choices. Copying the behavior of another person could also cause confusion about your own identity. On the other hand, modeling your behavior after the positive traits of others can sometimes result in strengthened character.

Story
Mighty Metalmark Moths

Mighty Metalmark Moths

The jumping spider likes making a meal out of moths. So it's pretty easy to understand why most moths panic when they see these spiders. The scared moths try to fly away. But the jumping spider is quick. Most of the time, the moths end up as lunch.

The metalmark moth is different, though. Instead of taking off, it stays put. This moth is small but gutsy. It stands its ground. The metalmark moth flares out its back wings and holds its front wings above its body at an angle. Sometimes the metalmark moth even dances *toward* the spider.

Do you think the moth's actions sound brave? Or do they just sound dangerous? Maybe it's a bit of both. But the metalmark moth has a secret. It's one of nature's most skillful copycats.

The metalmark moth's colors are similar to the jumping spider's markings. When the moth holds up its wings, it imitates the shape of the jumping spider. And when the moth dances toward the spider in a jumping, jerking way, it is copying the way a jumping spider moves. It's a tricky moth in spider's clothing.

These tricks confuse most spiders. Jumping spiders have good eyesight. But it's not good enough to spot the moth's trick right away. For a few seconds, the spider isn't sure if it's looking at a friend, a foe, or food.

The spider isn't confused for long. It soon catches on to the moth's disguise. But usually, the spider hesitates long enough for the moth to flit away. The spider misses out on a tasty lunch. And the metalmark moth sheds its disguise— until it meets another jumping spider.

From *Building Character with True Stories from Nature* by Barbara A. Lewis, copyright © 2012. Free Spirit Publishing Inc., Minneapolis, MN; 800-735-7323; www.freespirit.com. This page may be reproduced for use within an individual classroom. For all other uses, contact www.freespirit.com/company/permissions.cfm.

Talk It Over

Use these questions to guide your students in considering analogies between metalmark moths and courage, fairness, and other character traits and behaviors in people.

Compare the metalmark moth's ability to copy a jumping spider to people who copy the habits of others.

- If you copy negative behaviors such as lying, cheating, or being rude to others, you might not feel good about yourself. These traits might become habits. You might get in trouble.

- If you copy positive character traits such as honesty, helpfulness, respect, and courage, you can learn to be a person with stronger character and more positive habits.

What might happen if you copy another person even when it goes against the voice inside you?

- Showing integrity means acting according to your beliefs. But if you are not true to your own good values and to yourself, you might make poor decisions. You could also start to get confused about who you really are.

- It is good to have positive role models. Mimicking good behavior can help you strengthen positive character traits. But it's still important to stay true to yourself and to be genuine. You don't have to change the person you are to improve your character habits.

- Copying good behavior is not the same as copying another person's homework, test, or ideas. It's never the right decision to take credit for someone else's work. It is not fair to that person or to other people who are doing the work without copying.

The metalmark moth stands up to the jumping spider. Can you make a comparison to a person standing up to someone who is bullying others?

- The moth is small, but he makes himself look big to the spider. Sometimes people can do that by showing confidence and strength.

- It takes courage to stand up for someone else when you see a person being treated unfairly.

- Sometimes you need to get help from an adult. It's not always safe to confront someone who is bullying others. Use your good judgment, and remember that getting help is still a positive step.

Metalmark Moth Facts

Unlike many other moths, metalmark moths are active during the day.

Metalmark moths get their name from the iridescent patches that many of these moths have on their wings, which are metallic in appearance.

One study found that the jumping spider only catches and eats 6 percent of the metalmark moths it encounters, compared to more than 60 percent of moths in general.

The metalmark moth doesn't fly away when it faces danger. Can you compare this bold behavior to standing up for your own values and what you believe?

- It can take courage to stand up for what you believe, especially if others might make fun of you for doing so. But each time you do this, you get a little stronger. It may be easier next time.

- When you choose not to steal, lie, or cheat even when others are pressuring you to do so, you become a stronger person. It takes a lot of courage to stand up to peer pressure, especially if it is coming from people you think of as your friends.

- When you don't use bad language around people who do talk that way, you are standing up for what you believe.

Sometimes, the moth *does* get eaten by the spider. Can you make an analogy between this risk and dangerous situations that people might be in?

- It's important to protect yourself in dangerous situations. Being careful doesn't mean you're not brave.

- Sometimes people get away with risky behavior. But that doesn't mean they will always be safe if they continue that behavior. For example, someone might cheat on a test once without anyone knowing. But the next time, he or she might get caught and be in big trouble.

Activities

Activity 1: Feelings Charades

Materials
Slips of paper with feelings words written on them
Hat, box, or other container

Preparation
Before doing this activity, write feelings words on slips of paper, fold them in half, and put them in a container. Suggestions for feelings words include: *discouraged, happy, loving, confused, frightened.*

Directions
Play Feelings Charades. Have kids take turns drawing slips and acting out emotions without using any words. Give the group a set amount of time (for example, two or three minutes) to guess the feeling. Like the metalmark moth tricks the jumping spider, can you trick people as to how you really feel?

Allow as many students to act as you have time for, while still leaving time for discussion after the game. Then talk about how easy or difficult students found it to guess the feelings correctly. Are some people easier to read than others? Are some types of feelings harder to identify than others?

Extend the discussion to consider whether it's a good idea to hide our emotions. Should we always show people how we really feel? Why or why not? Explore ideas of honesty and integrity with the group.

Activity 2: Character Cartoons

Materials
Paper
Crayons, colored pencils, markers, or paints

Directions
Ask kids to write and illustrate cartoon drawings about metalmark moths standing up to jumping spiders, and to tell a story about bullying, courage, or being true to oneself. Assure them that they don't need to create timeless works of art; the main thing is to explore some of the lesson's ideas in a creative way. If desired, allow them to pair up and cooperate on these cartoons. Invite them to title their finished works with slogans related to the cartoon's theme. For example, "It isn't big to make others feel small."

After kids are finished, invite those who feel comfortable doing so to share their cartoons with the group. Talk about the different ideas and stories that the kids came up with.

Activity 3: Character Copycats

Materials
Character Container handout (on CD-ROM)
Kid-safe scissors
Glue sticks, school glue, or tape
Colored pencils, crayons, or markers
Small strips of paper

Directions
Pass out copies of the Character Container handout and help kids make their envelopes. Ask them to write their names on their envelopes and give them some time to decorate them. Place all the envelopes on a shelf, table, or other space in your room.

Next, hand out several strips of paper to each student. Ask kids to think of positive character traits—traits that other people could try to copy to improve their own character habits—shown by the people sitting on their right and left. Have each kid write the name of the person they're describing on one side of a slip of paper, and the good character trait on the other. For example, the student is caring, courageous, or honest. Remind students that only positive traits are allowed. Insist on an atmosphere of respect and kindness.

Collect all the papers and put them in the correct envelopes. (As you do this, make sure the traits are all positive. Discard any that aren't.) Do this every day for a week, changing the system each time so that students aren't describing the same classmates as they did the day before. At the end of the week, give kids their envelopes and let them open them to see what's inside.

If kids feel comfortable doing so, allow them to read some of the traits out loud. Talk about each one. Ask kids if there are some traits they wish were stronger in themselves. Talk about how to be good character copycats and how to choose positive role models. Then give the whole group a round of applause for all their good behavior!

Lesson 17
Oleanders

Character Key Words
Honesty • Safety • Integrity • Respect

Students will
- learn about the beautiful but poisonous oleander plant and discover reasons to respect this flower's place in nature
- compare and contrast the beauty and poison of oleander blossoms to human qualities of honesty and deception
- talk about how mixing apples and carrots with oleander leaves is analogous to mixing the truth with a few lies, or positive behavior with a little bit of negative behavior
- create and apply analogies between animals that are immune to oleander's poison and people who get used to negative habits

Overview
The blossoms of the oleander plant are beautiful—and they contain a deadly poison. This contrast will give you and your students a good starting point for discussions about appearance and how looks can be deceiving. You can extend this analogy in the opposite direction by considering the idea that, although oleander's poison makes it unsafe to eat, the plant also has disease-fighting properties that make it deserving of respect as a part of nature.

In the story, kids will also learn that oleander leaves taste bitter, but that mixing them with something sweet can disguise the poison's flavor. This fact is good fodder for making analogies to a person who mixes truth with small lies that may go undetected. In addition, some animals seem to have developed a resistance to oleander poison. Your students can consider how this resistance is similar to the way people can get used to negative behavior over time. Similarly, they can see that practicing positive character habits can become a habit, as well.

Story
Pretty, Poisonous Oleanders

Pretty, Poisonous Oleanders

Owners of a farm in California woke up one morning to an awful sight. Twenty-three of their horses were very sick. Someone had climbed over the farm's gate and fed oleander leaves to the horses. These leaves are very poisonous. So why did the horses eat them? Whoever poisoned the horses mixed the leaves with apples and carrots. Most of the time, animals know which plants to avoid. Their instincts tell them to steer clear of dangerous foods. But the sweet taste of apples and carrots tricked the horses. The horses could have died from the poison. But their owners moved fast. They got help right away, and all the horses got better.

Oleander doesn't *look* dangerous. The bushes show off flashy blossoms in white, pink, red, purple, yellow, or orange. The flowers smell fresh and sweet like spring. Their scent is used in some perfumes.

But every part of the oleander plant is poisonous, including its blossoms. The poison can cause stomachaches and throwing up. It can lead to heart problems, brain problems, or even death. And a person doesn't have to eat the plant to get sick. Just breathing in the smoke from burning oleander can be dangerous.

Not all animals seem to mind the oleander's poison. It doesn't hurt some caterpillars, butterflies, rodents, and birds. Maybe these creatures have built up a resistance to the plant. Maybe they don't eat enough to get sick. Or maybe their bodies change the poison into something safe.

From *Building Character with True Stories from Nature* by Barbara A. Lewis, copyright © 2012. Free Spirit Publishing Inc., Minneapolis, MN; 800-735-7323; www.freespirit.com. This page may be reproduced for use within an individual classroom. For all other uses, contact www.freespirit.com/company/permissions.cfm.

And oleander has a good side, too. For about 1,500 years, people have used oleander to help fight sickness and treat injuries. Some doctors think the plant can treat snake bites. It might also help fight skin cancer and other diseases.

But many people still fear oleander. Lots of scary stories tell of oleander poisoning. One is a ghost story. The tale takes place at Myrtles Plantation in Louisiana. Many people say this place is haunted. This old plantation is a hotel now, and some people like to stay there and get scared. One of the Myrtles Plantation's most famous ghosts is called Chloe. According to the legends, Chloe was a slave at the home in the 1800s. Chloe's master treated her very badly. He even ordered that one of her ears be cut off. Chloe wanted to punish him. So when she baked a cake for the family, Chloe changed the recipe. She added oleander leaves to the cake. The poison killed Chloe's master's wife and children, but the master never ate any of the cake. Chloe paid for her crime with her life. Now people say that Chloe's ghost haunts the old house.

Is Chloe's tale true? Are there such things as ghosts? Was Chloe even a real person? Many history experts think the whole story is made up. But one thing is for sure: it's best not to get too friendly with the oleander plant.

From *Building Character with True Stories from Nature* by Barbara A. Lewis, copyright © 2012. Free Spirit Publishing Inc., Minneapolis, MN; 800-735-7323; www.freespirit.com. This page may be reproduced for use within an individual classroom. For all other uses, contact www.freespirit.com/company/permissions.cfm.

Talk It Over

Use these questions to guide your students in considering analogies between oleanders and safety, integrity, and other character traits and behaviors in people.

Mixing apples and carrots with oleander can sweeten the bitter taste of the poisonous leaves. Can you make an analogy to people who are honest or dishonest?

- If someone mostly tells the truth but sometimes mixes in a few lies, it's easy to be fooled. The truth "sweetens" the lie, so that it becomes hard to tell what is true and what is false.

- If you let yourself be dishonest some of the time, you might eventually get used to it. You might lower your own standards.

- Half-truths, fibs, and "white lies" are still dishonest. Always try to tell the truth.

- If you watch movies or play games that have violent or scary parts, you might excuse those parts because you like the rest of the movie or game.

The farm owners in "Pretty, Poisonous Oleanders" had to act quickly to save their horses. Can you think of other times when acting quickly might save something or someone?

- Sometimes when you have a disagreement with someone else, talking it through right away can keep it from becoming a bigger problem. Or if you realize that you've hurt someone, it's best to apologize as soon as you can. If you wait too long, anger, misunderstanding, and hurt feelings can grow stronger.

- If you are sick or hurt, the sooner you take care of it, the sooner you'll start to feel better.

- If you catch yourself cheating, lying, or making other poor choices, try to stop as soon as you can. If you don't stop early, it can get easier and easier to do these things.

- Speak up if you think you or someone else might be in danger. If you wait, it might be too late to help.

The oleander bush has beautiful blossoms and looks harmless. Are there situations that people might get into that seem safe at first but are actually dangerous?

- It's never a good idea to go anywhere with a stranger, even if he or she seems nice.

- You might go to a party that sounds fun and then find out that kids there are doing risky things, such as smoking, drinking alcohol, or using drugs. If that happens, call a parent or another grown-up to pick you up and take you home.

Caterpillars, moths, and some rodents and birds seem to be immune to the oleander's poison. Can you make an analogy to behaviors in people?

- It is possible to build up immunity (get used to) disrespect, lying, bad language, and other poor behavior by doing it over and over, or by seeing it over and over. Maybe at first you feel bad about doing or seeing these things. But after a while, they don't bother you as much as they used to. It's better to avoid these behaviors in the beginning. And if you do find yourself making poor character choices, you can try to stop right away.

- You can build up a tolerance for poor character patterns by taking part in them, or by watching them. But you can also build up a habit of good character by making small, positive choices each day.

The oleander's appearance is deceiving. It's beautiful, but also poisonous. At the same time, even though it's unsafe to eat, it might help us treat some sicknesses. Can you draw an analogy between these contrasts and human nature?

- No one is all bad or all good. Every person has positive *and* negative traits. And we can all work on making better choices and building our positive character habits.

- It's best not to make assumptions about a person based on just one of his or her traits. Get to know someone before you draw conclusions about his or her character.

- Everyone deserves respect.

Oleander Facts

Oleander (also called Nerium oleander) has been used in folk medicine and by herbalists for more than 1,500 years.

Oleander bushes can grow to be more than 20 feet tall.

Because oleander grows well in warm, dry climates, it is a very popular plant in landscaping, despite its poisonous qualities.

Activities

Activity 1: Hidden in Plain Sight

Materials
Hidden in Plain Sight handout (on CD-ROM)
Optional: Colored pencils

Directions
Pass out copies of the Hidden in Plain Sight handout and invite kids to spend some time hunting for the hidden objects. If desired, kids can color them in as they find them. As kids work, talk about how easy or hard it is to spot the hidden pictures. Point out that it is easy to miss these pictures unless you are looking for them. Even then, you might not see some of them. Make an analogy to the oleander leaves mixed with sweet foods. Is it also easy to overlook or stop

noticing negative behavior if you are only looking at the big picture?

To further explain this idea, present the following hypothetical situation to students and talk with them about the questions it raises:

Your best friend often tells small lies. You care about your friend a lot, and the two of you have fun together. But you know that lying is wrong. What should you do? If you do nothing, will you eventually stop noticing the lies? Will your friend try to get away with bigger lies? How will you know whether your friend is telling *you* the truth or not?

Activity 2: Small Acts and Big Results

Materials
Milk (2% or whole)
Soup bowl or other broad, shallow dish
Red, yellow, green, and blue food coloring
Liquid dish soap
Cotton swabs

Directions
Pour enough milk into the dish to cover the bottom completely. The milk should be about ¼-inch deep. Near the center of the dish, add a drop of each food coloring: red, yellow, green, and blue.

Next, dab the end of a cotton swab into a little bit of dish soap. Put the soapy end into the middle of the milk and food coloring. Hold it there for about 10 to 15 seconds. Suddenly the colors in the milk will start moving, swirling together and outward.

Compare this phenomenon to the idea that a small act can have big consequences—bad or good. A negative habit can soon become hard to break. A tiny lie can quickly spread. And a situation that seems safe can sometimes become dangerous in a hurry. Talk with kids about how they can deal with all of these situations. Discuss various related scenarios and brainstorm positive responses to them.

Note: The secret behind this demonstration is in the tiny drop of soap. Dish soap weakens the chemical bonds holding the milk's proteins and fats together. The food coloring allows you to see this

process. For more details see: www.stevespangler
science.com/experiment/milk-color-explosion.

Activity 3: Seeds of Respect

Materials

Newspaper

Marigold seeds (4 to 6 per student)

Mini clay pots (1 per student)

Pebbles

Potting soil

Large tray(s) to hold pots

Construction paper, cut into pieces about 1 inch by
2 inches (1 per student)

Markers or crayons

Plastic straws (1 per student)

Tape or staples

Directions

Spread newspaper on your classroom floor or on a large work surface. Tell kids that you're going to plant marigolds and work on "growing" respect. Explain that oleander wouldn't be a good plant to grow in the classroom, but that marigolds are also pretty flowers that can remind us to show respect for others and ourselves.

Show kids how to plant their marigold seeds. First, place a few pebbles in the bottom of the pot to help the water drain from the soil. Then add enough potting soil to fill the pot up to about 2 inches from the top. Sprinkle the seeds on the soil and add another half inch of soil.

Note: Instead of clay pots, you can use 16-ounce biodegradable plastic cups or reuse clean cottage cheese containers or other containers of similar size. If you use plastic, be sure to poke a few holes in the bottom of each container before using. Whatever you plant the seeds in, start a couple of extra plants in case some kids' seeds don't germinate.

Assist any kids who need help planting their marigold seeds. While they work, talk about how respect can grow just like a flower. Discuss the ways that positive and negative behaviors and character habits are related to respect, both for themselves and for others. For example, if you respect your teacher, you do your homework on time. If you respect your family, you help keep your home clean. If you respect others, you are polite to them. If you respect yourself, you take good care of your health. Help kids brainstorm other ways of growing respect, and invite them to talk about possible causes and effects of respectful (and disrespectful) actions.

When all kids have planted their seeds, have each kid write a way to be respectful on a piece of construction paper. (If some kids have trouble fitting their messages on the paper, you can write for them.) Then help each student tape or staple his or her piece of paper to one end of a plastic straw, resembling a flag. Kids can then plant these respect flags in their pots.

Finally, place all the pots in a tray near a window.

Talk about how kids will need to care for their plants by watering them. Compare this to the way being respectful is a habit and takes practice. If we work to care for it, respect can grow and grow.

Lesson 18
Parrots

Character Key Words
Adaptability • Communication • Playfulness • Wisdom and Learning

Students will
- learn about parrots, including the fact that they are highly intelligent, are good at mimicking human voices and words, and have a playful and sometimes bold nature
- compare parrots that mimic human voices to people who mimic others as a form of bullying
- consider a comparison between the parrots' adaptability and skill in learning and saying words (despite the fact that they have no vocal cords) to people who develop new skills and adapt to new situations
- draw connections between Willie's rescue warning and people who discover skills or courage they didn't know they had

Overview
Parrots are well known for their ability to mimic human words. Some African gray parrots have learned to recognize up to 1,000 words and to say over 100 words. This talent is especially impressive because parrots do not have vocal cords. Parrots also amuse and entertain people, learning tricks and repeating words that get a laugh or a reaction.

Along with this adaptability and high intelligence comes an attitude. Parrots are playful and fun. They can also be very demanding, and they sometimes repeat annoying words endlessly. But they make popular pets. They seem to connect easily with humans, and often build strong and lasting relationships with their owners.

Story
Playful Parrots

Playful Parrots

Have you ever seen a parrot at a soccer game? Probably not. It's not a common sight. But a Senegalese parrot named Me-Tu is a great soccer fan. He and his owner go to soccer games in Northern Ireland. Me-Tu can copy sounds he hears. He learned to copy the sound of the referee's whistle. But it got him into trouble. When Me-Tu whistled, everyone thought it was the referee's whistle. The game stopped. On the field, the players scratched their heads and looked confused. And Me-Tu just kept whistling. Each time he did, he stopped the game again. Finally the referee figured out the problem. He red-carded Me-Tu and kicked the pesky parrot right out of the stadium.

Parrots can copy other sounds, too. Many are great at mimicking human voices. But parrots don't have any vocal cords. So how do they talk? To make sound, parrots push air across a special part of their throat.

African gray parrots are very good at learning words. Alex was a famous African gray. His trainer taught him to say more than 150 words. Alex could name colors and pick out shapes. He learned to count up to six, and even to add up numbers. Alex's trainer said the parrot was as smart as a five- or six-year-old child. Not all experts agree. But everyone could see that Alex was definitely bird-brained—in a *good* way!

From *Building Character with True Stories from Nature* by Barbara A. Lewis, copyright © 2012. Free Spirit Publishing Inc., Minneapolis, MN; 800-735-7323; www.freespirit.com. This page may be reproduced for use within an individual classroom. For all other uses, contact www.freespirit.com/company/permissions.cfm.

Along with high intelligence, parrots can have big attitudes. They are very loud. They love attention. They demand toys and snacks. Sometimes they keep repeating a bad behavior. It's almost as if they're *trying* to annoy you. And they seem to like getting a big reaction. So be careful what you say around a smart parrot. They often repeat naughty words over and over.

Parrots are also good at learning tricks. Over the years parrots have entertained many people. They swing on parrot-size swings. They hop through hoops and untie shoelaces. They ride tiny tricycles.

Some parrots even dance! Snowball is a cockatoo. He boogies to popular songs. Millions of people have watched Snowball strutting and swaying in videos online. Snowball stomps his clawed feet. He bounces his head to the music's beat. He even ends his performance by bowing to the camera over and over.

Scientists say Snowball's sense of rhythm is big news. They were surprised to learn that birds could move to the beat of music. They had thought that only people could do that. Snowball helped change their minds.

Another parrot star is a Quaker parrot named Willie. He isn't a performer like Snowball. But he sure earned his owner's love and admiration. One day Willie's owner was babysitting a two-year-old girl named Hannah. While Hannah was eating breakfast, the babysitter left Willie and the little girl alone for a moment. Suddenly, Hannah choked on some food. She stopped breathing and turned blue. But Willie came to the rescue. He screamed very loudly and rattled his cage. He yelled, "Mama, baby," again and again. Right away, the babysitter rushed to Hannah and saved her. If Willie hadn't made so much noise, Hannah might have died. The babysitter was very surprised. She had never heard Willie use the word "baby" that way before. Other people admired Willie for his actions, too. The local Red Cross gave him an award for his heroic act. They named him an official Animal Lifesaver.

From *Building Character with True Stories from Nature* by Barbara A. Lewis, copyright © 2012. Free Spirit Publishing Inc., Minneapolis, MN; 800-735-7323; www.freespirit.com. This page may be reproduced for use within an individual classroom. For all other uses, contact www.freespirit.com/company/permissions.cfm.

Talk It Over

Use these questions to guide your students in considering analogies between parrots and learning, adaptability, and other character traits and behaviors in people.

Although many examples of parrots mimicking human voices are funny, it's not always funny for us to mimic other people. When is it not nice or not funny for people to copy others?

- If someone copies another person's gestures or voice in order to put him or her down, it can embarrass and hurt the other person.

- Mimicking another person's voice in a joking way can be a form of bullying. It may start out as a joke, but it can quickly grow into something much more hurtful and serious. For example, if you mimic another person's voice or actions in a mocking way, that behavior can spread to other people.

- If you copy someone else, it can hurt you, too. After a while you might feel like you're forgetting who you really are. It's better to create your own voice and personality than to be a copy of someone else.

Can you make an analogy between parrots that learn to speak without vocal cords and people who learn new skills and adapt to new situations?

- People who are injured or who are born without certain abilities can learn new skills and lead very productive lives. For example, Stephen Hawking is a great scientist. He suffers from a disease that makes him unable to have control of his muscles. But Hawking has adapted. He has a special wheelchair, and he communicates with a voice synthesizer. Another example of adaptability is Mike McNaughton. He stepped on a landmine in Afghanistan in 2002, losing his right leg. After recovering from his injuries, he became an avid runner and bicyclist. He even went for a jog with President George W. Bush. McNaughton has also worked to help other injured war veterans.

- Most kids have trouble with some subjects in school. Instead of giving up on those subjects, they can try to get extra help from the teacher or a tutor.

- Someone might love music, but not enjoy singing. He or she could learn to dance, play a musical instrument, or write songs instead.

- Moving to a new town or a new school can be hard. Adapting to a different place and making new friends is harder for some people than it is for others. But everyone can practice and improve on these skills. And that will make it easier to adjust the next time there's a big change.

Parrots can be demanding, and they love attention. Can you make an analogy to the behavior of people?

- Sometimes people want to be the center of attention. At times, this can get boring or annoying, like a parrot repeating words over and over. But we don't always know *why* people demand attention. They may feel bad about themselves, or they may feel that no one cares about them. It's important not to judge others or make assumptions about them.

- Giving attention to a behavior will often reinforce it. Getting a big reaction, whether it's laughter or disgust, can lead people to repeat a behavior over and over.

Parrots can be playful and mischievous. Their behavior can be funny, but sometimes they get in trouble, too—like Me-Tu at the soccer game. Can you think of ways to compare this characteristic to people?

- Everyone needs to play. Playing helps us have fun, be creative, and make new friends. It can even make us healthier.

- Sometimes too much playing can get in the way of doing homework, chores, or other necessary tasks. It's important to balance your work time and your play time. Sometimes learning how to reach this balance takes time and practice.

- People don't all think that the same things are fun, or funny. Everyone is different. It's important to respect other people's feelings.

Parrots are very skilled at learning tricks. They seem to be good at solving puzzles, too. Can you make an analogy to people learning new things?

- You can learn new skills and get better at them if you practice.

- Learning new ideas and facts is fun and interesting.

- Your brain is like a muscle. The more you use it, the stronger it gets.

Some kinds of parrots learn words, and Alex the gray parrot seemed to understand how to communicate with his trainer. How do people communicate?

- Learning to communicate well takes practice. True communication only happens when people understand each other. One way to communicate better is by trying to imagine how the other person feels. This is called compassion or empathy.

- There are many ways to communicate. Talking is just one of them. People also communicate with their facial expressions and their gestures. You can also communicate with other people through writing, drawing, or singing.

- People in different places use different languages. People with hearing impairment use sign language. It can be challenging to learn another language. But it's fun and rewarding to be able to communicate with others.

Willie the parrot turned out to be an unlikely hero. Can you make a comparison between his story and people who become heroes?

- Heroes aren't always obvious. You probably can't look around in a classroom and say, "Oh, I see a hero over there." But that doesn't mean that heroes aren't around you. And you may be a hero yourself. Courage can come from unexpected people and show up in unexpected situations.

- People who become heroes are often ordinary people who stay brave just a little longer than others in a scary situation, or people who don't give up. Sometimes they discover courage and skills that they didn't know they had in order to rescue or help someone.

Parrot Facts

There are about 350 different kinds of parrots. Many kinds of parrots are endangered in the wild.

Many parrots have long life spans. Some can live to be 80 years old. In that time, they can form close relationships with people.

Parrots say words by pushing air across the mouth of the bifurcated trachea. They can make different sounds by changing the trachea's shape and depth.

Activities

Activity 1: Switch It Up

Materials
Soccer ball or kickball

Directions
Invite students to switch it up and see how adaptable they are. First have them try writing with their nondominant hands. Give them some time to have fun with this. Next, have each kid kick a ball with the opposite foot from what he or she would usually use.

Variation: You could also give students other challenges in this activity, such as playing guitar with opposite hands.

Afterward, talk with kids about the experience of switching their hands and feet. Did they find that the tasks they were doing got any easier after a little while? How long do kids think they would have to practice before they felt just as comfortable and skilled using their nondominant hands or feet for the same tasks? Do they think they would *ever* get to this point?

Expand the conversation to talk about adaptability. Why do kids think it can be difficult to adapt to change and new situations? What are some ways to increase our adaptability? Why can it be helpful to develop this positive trait?

Activity 2: New Words

Materials
None

Directions
Parrots are great at learning new words—and so are people! Have each student learn a few words in another language (for example, how to count to ten, or how to say hello and good-bye). Help kids choose their languages. Some overlap is fine, but try to have as wide a range of languages as is possible and realistic for your group. Help kids find the words they want to say and learn how to pronounce them correctly. Then give them a week or so to practice and memorize their words. If desired, you can set aside a little bit of time each day to work with kids on this activity.

When the week (or whatever amount of time you've allotted) is over, have every student say the words they've learned (along with the English meanings) in front of the class. Be sure to celebrate kids' efforts even if they don't get the pronunciation exactly right.

After kids have shared what they've learned, talk about their experience learning these new words. Was it fun? Challenging? Both? What did they like best about it? What did they find the most difficult? Why do they think it's important to be able to communicate with others, even if it takes some extra time or work? What are other skills that may be challenging but rewarding to learn?

Activity 3: What's It For?

Materials
What's It For? handout (on CD-ROM)

Directions
Pass out copies of the What's It For? handout. Ask kids to imagine that they've never seen any of the items on the list before, and that they don't know what they are used for. Invite them to come up with a new use for each thing. For example, kids could imagine that a shovel is for cooking food over a campfire, or that a fork is used for combing hair.

Encourage kids to be really playful and creative with this activity. They can fill in the handout individually and then share their ideas, or you can brainstorm as a group. Either way, keep this activity fun, light, and full of laughter. Talk about how ideas that seem silly at first can turn out to be amazing. Some of the world's greatest inventions sounded nutty or impossible at the time. And many inventions have been created by changing the form or the use of an item that already exists. Discuss how people can also change their interests and talents by thinking of different ways to express or use them.

If you like, extend the conversation to encourage kids to consider what it would be like if they'd *really* never seen a shovel or a fork, for example. What would they think when they first encountered one? Talk about how it can be hard to make sense of something new and unfamiliar. Everyone is confused or uncertain at times. We should never be afraid to ask questions. That's how we learn and strengthen our minds.

Lesson 19
Penguins

Character Key Words
Responsibility • Cooperation • Loyalty

Students will

- learn about penguins, including the fact that there are many different species and that they have unique characteristics
- compare the responsibility that penguins take in caring for their young to responsibilities that people have
- make analogies between the cooperation that exists among penguins and cooperation among people

Overview

Movies and books about penguins have helped make them much-loved creatures, famous for their tuxedo-like feathers and waddling walks. But penguins are more than just celebrity birds. They have many interesting behaviors that can serve as starting points for analogies to human character traits. For example, Adélie penguins mate for life, demonstrating lasting loyalty. And many penguins, including emperor penguins, share the responsibility of rearing their chicks. Penguin mates—and whole penguin communities—cooperate to keep themselves, the eggs, and the chicks warm and safe in Antarctica's cold, windy conditions.

But it isn't all work and no play for penguins. They can also be curious, spirited, and playful.

Story

Penguin Partners

Penguin Partners

With their tuxedo-like feathers and waddling walk, penguins are popular birds. Many books and movies feature penguins. Maybe you have seen cartoon penguins thumping their toes on the ice in the *Happy Feet* movies. Maybe you saw real penguins making their long trip in *March of the Penguins.* Or you might have read about these birds in *Mr. Popper's Penguins.*

There are many different kinds of penguins. The biggest penguin in the world is the emperor penguin. A full-grown emperor can be 4 feet tall. It might weigh almost 100 pounds. That may be bigger than you!

Emperor penguin parents share the job of raising their chicks. The female penguin lays just one egg a year. Afterward, she needs food. She leaves to hunt and eat fish. She can be gone for two months or more. Meanwhile, the male holds the egg on his feet. He has to be very careful. Emperor penguins live in Antarctica. The winter is long and harsh. The male has to keep the egg off the ice. If the egg gets too cold, the chick inside will die. To stay warm, males huddle together. Thousands of them stand close to each other on the ice. The big group also helps protect the penguins from seals and other threats.

While the female is gone, the male has to stay with the egg all the time. He doesn't even get to eat. He may lose half his body weight. When the female comes back, the egg has hatched. Families find each other among thousands of other penguins by making little trilling, honking noises. Each penguin in the family recognizes these sounds.

When they find each other, the penguin parents trade places. The male goes hunting. And the female keeps the little chick safe and warm.

The Adélie penguin is another kind of penguin. It's one of the smallest penguins. It's only about 27 inches tall. It weighs just 8 to 12 pounds. Adélie penguins mate for life. Like many other penguins, the males and females take turns caring for the eggs. When chicks hatch, their parents feed them tasty dinners of fish and krill (tiny, shrimplike animals).

From *Building Character with True Stories from Nature* by Barbara A. Lewis, copyright © 2012. Free Spirit Publishing Inc., Minneapolis, MN; 800-735-7323; www.freespirit.com. This page may be reproduced for use within an individual classroom. For all other uses, contact www.freespirit.com/company/permissions.cfm.

Adélie and emperor penguins are both good swimmers. But the little Adélie can go much faster. Especially when it's in danger, the Adélie can swim circles around the emperor penguin. And on land, the little Adélie is also much quicker and more nimble. Out of the water, the big emperor is a bit clumsy.

Like other penguins, Adélie penguins work hard to care for their young. They also seem to love playing. They slide down icy hills on their stomachs. Their long black feathers hang down like coattails behind them. Adélie penguins are curious, too. When people show up, Adélies don't act afraid. They'll march right up to cameras to check them out. They've even stared down dogs.

Even though they already look like they're wearing suits, penguins need special outfits sometimes. Pierre is an African penguin. He lives at an aquarium in San Francisco. Pierre is more than twenty-five years old. That's very old for a penguin. But a while ago, he had a problem. He was going bald on parts of his body. That's bad news for a penguin. Pierre needed his feathers to keep warm. So experts at the aquarium had an idea. They had a special, penguin-size wetsuit made for Pierre. It would keep him warm until his feathers grew back. But there was still one big question. Would the other birds accept Pierre's new look?

The answer was yes. His fellow penguins swam near him. They didn't seem to care about his wetsuit. And soon enough, Pierre was back in the pool, splashing and swimming with the rest of the penguins.

From *Building Character with True Stories from Nature* by Barbara A. Lewis, copyright © 2012. Free Spirit Publishing Inc., Minneapolis, MN; 800-735-7323; www.freespirit.com. This page may be reproduced for use within an individual classroom. For all other uses, contact www.freespirit.com/company/permissions.cfm.

Talk It Over

Use these questions to guide your students in considering analogies between penguins and loyalty, cooperation, and other character traits and behaviors in people.

The emperor penguin is the world's largest penguin. But Adélie penguins, which are some of the smallest penguins, are faster and more nimble than the big emperors. Can you make an analogy to people who have individual strengths and talents regardless of size or appearance?

- It isn't always the biggest or toughest-looking person who is the most athletic, the most skilled, or the bravest.

- It's best not to make assumptions about a person's character or talents based on what he or she looks like.

- If you're willing to work hard and keep trying, you can reach almost any goal you set for yourself.

- It is the drive inside you—not the way you look—that makes you succeed.

Male and female penguins share the responsibility of hatching their eggs and raising their chicks. If both partners didn't do their share, the young penguins would not survive. Can you make an analogy between this and the responsibilities people have?

- Parents and family members share responsibilities in caring for children. Different family members may earn money, prepare meals, and so on. Kids also have responsibilities. They help their families with household chores and other tasks.

- In every area of life, people have different responsibilities. All of these different responsibilities are important. They help keep things running smoothly in families, homes, companies, communities, and countries.

- Everyone in a classroom has responsibilities. The classroom works better if everyone does his or her job.

Penguin Facts

When emperor penguins huddle together for warmth, they can temporarily increase the temperature within the huddle from sub-zero to over 90 degrees Fahrenheit.

The world's smallest penguin is called the little penguin or little blue penguin. It stands just 13 inches high and weighs around 3 pounds.

Adélie penguins sometimes swim more than 150 miles round-trip while hunting for food.

Penguins cooperate to stay warm in Antarctica's bitter cold. Can you make a comparison with people who cooperate to do jobs or reach goals?

- Families may cooperate by assigning different chores to different family members. That way, all the chores get done and no one has to do all the work.

- Cooperation often helps a job get done faster and better. For example, students working together on a project might each be responsible for a different part of the project depending on their strengths. The student who loves drawing can make a poster, while the person who enjoys facts and figures can gather some of the research.

Adélie penguins mate for life. They remain loyal to their partners as long as they live. And Pierre's fellow penguins didn't seem to mind that he looked different from them in his wetsuit. Can you make an analogy to loyalty among people?

- If you are loyal to your family members, you stick together and support each other—no matter what happens.

- If you are loyal to your friends, you stick up for each other, no matter what anyone says. But loyalty can also mean having the courage to tell a friend that you're worried he or she is making a mistake or practicing a habit that might be harmful.

- You should always know what you are being loyal to. Before you promise your loyalty to people, groups, or causes, it's important to find out what they believe and what they stand for.

- Loyalty goes beyond appearances. You're loyal to your friends and family because of who they are inside, not what they look like.

Penguins work hard to care for their eggs and their chicks, sometimes in very harsh conditions. But penguins also seem to have fun. They appear to enjoy playing and sliding on the ice and snow. Can you make a comparison to people?

- If you only work, you can feel stressed. If you only play, you don't learn and grow as much as you could. Everyone needs balance in his or her life.

- Part of the reason penguins are so popular with people is because they seem to be so fun and playful. If you have fun and have a positive attitude—both when you're working and when you're playing—people usually enjoy being around you.

Activities

Activity 1: Responsibility Roster

Materials
Responsibility Roster handout (on CD-ROM)
Stickers (penguins, gold stars, or other)

Directions
Create a classroom Responsibility Roster. As a group, brainstorm the jobs that need to be done each day in the classroom. (For example, watering plants or turning out the lights.) Decide who will do each job first, and then choose a fair way to rotate the jobs. Remind kids that not everyone will have a job every day, but that they all have responsibility in keeping the classroom a clean, safe, fun place where everyone can learn.

Fill out the Responsibility Roster handout (either in pen/pencil or on a computer) with your classroom responsibilities and the names of the students assigned to carry out these jobs. If necessary, you can use more than one chart.

Tell kids that when a job is done on time, the student responsible for that job will get a sticker in his or her box on the Responsibility Roster. If the job is not done on time, the box will be left empty.

At the end of each week, look at your Responsibility Roster as a group. See how many stickers and how many empty spaces you have. Avoid placing blame on any individual. Instead, keep the focus on how responsibly you acted as a group, and how you could do even better. How does getting these jobs done help the whole class?

Activity 2: Good Guides

Materials
Masking tape or sidewalk chalk to mark two paths
Large open space for constructing the paths (inside or outside)
Bandanas or other blindfolds (one for every two kids)

Preparation
Before beginning this activity, mark out two separate paths on the floor or the ground using tape or chalk. Depending on the ages and abilities of your group, you can make these paths as challenging as is appropriate, with zigzags and detours around simple (and safe) obstacles. However, try to make the paths of equal difficulty.

Directions
Divide your group into pairs. Then place the pairs in two teams, assigning each team to one of the paths. Blindfold one child from each pair. The partner who

can see has to guide the blindfolded partner along the path. He or she must do this only with words, not by physically leading or moving the partner. Each pair gets one "freebie"—one chance to go outside the lines of the path. If they go outside a second time, they're eliminated. Each pair that reaches the end of the path wins one point for their team. The team with the highest number of points wins. (Or you may choose not to have winners.)

After one round, switch partners so everyone has a chance to be guided and to guide. If you have time, you could also give each team a chance to try the other path.

Variation: You can also play this game without points and teams. Simply challenge the kids to try to reach the paths' ends.

Afterward, talk with kids about the activity. What was it like to be the guide? What was it like to be the person being guided? How did they need to work together to reach the end of the path? Did the blindfolded person have to trust his or her guide? How did that feel? Did the guides feel that they had a big responsibility as they kept their partners on track?

Activity 3: Find the Leader, Follow the Leader

Materials
None

Directions
Ask the kids to stand in a circle. For the first round, you be the leader. Let kids know that at some point you'll pass the leadership on to someone else—but that you'll do so without speaking. Maybe you'll nod your head in the direction of a student, or wink at him or her.

Start the game by demonstrating an action, such as nodding your head, clapping, or snapping your fingers. All the kids must follow what the leader is doing, repeating his or her actions. Each time the leader changes his or her action, everyone else changes their actions, too.

At any time, the leader can choose another leader, but he or she must do so silently. The new leader models a new action, and the old leader follows.

When leadership changes, kids can cooperate to let each other know who the new leader is. They can signal others by nodding in the direction of the new leader. See how long it takes for everyone to recognize him or her.

As kids play this game, they will hone their skills in nonverbal communication and cooperation. After playing for a while, talk about what kids thought of the experience. Was it hard to spot the new leader? Did kids get better at it, or at signaling others, during the course of the game? Did they feel any responsibility to pay attention to the leader? Why or why not? Did they cooperate to let others know when the leadership changed? If so, how?

Activity 4: Penguin Tunes

Materials
None

Directions
Invite kids to write songs about penguins and character. Show students how to make lists of words that rhyme, such as:

Penguin: *grin, fin, spin, jump in*
Cooperate: *great, wait, skate, trait*

Encourage kids to focus on positive character traits in their songs. They might write about how penguins work together to care for chicks, or about their playfulness. Invite kids to share their songs with the group.

Variation: Compose a single song as a group. Learn it and perform it for family and friends.

Lesson 20
Pigs

Character Key Words

Courage • Respect • Tolerance and Acceptance • Problem Solving • Wisdom and Learning

Students will

- learn facts about pigs that may surprise them, including that pigs are very intelligent and that some kinds of pigs make good pets
- compare the courage shown by a pig named LuLu with people who show courage to help someone or something
- make an analogy between the false ideas that people sometimes have about pigs and the false assumptions that people might make about each other

Overview

Pigs have long had a bad reputation—but that reputation isn't true or fair. Many people don't realize, for instance, that pigs are highly intelligent. In fact, they seem to have an amazing ability to size up a situation and solve a problem. In addition, contrary to what many people believe, pigs are not naturally dirty or smelly. Since pigs have no sweat glands, their bodies don't give off sweaty odors. And their habit of wallowing in the mud is actually a way to stay cool and healthy.

Kids will enjoy learning more about pigs and dispelling the assumptions they may have had about these animals. Considering these misperceptions is a great starting point for discussion about how people sometimes misjudge each other and about the value of keeping an open mind and respecting all people. And the story of LuLu, a potbellied pig that saved her owner's life, will capture kids' imaginations and inspire lively and meaningful conversation about courage and the many ways it can be shown.

Story

Problem-Solving Pigs

Problem-Solving Pigs

Unlike Wilbur, the "radiant" pig in the book *Charlotte's Web*, pigs don't really talk. But they *are* smart. And they're good problem solvers. One farmer in Australia found out just how good pigs are at figuring out puzzles. He was having trouble keeping one clever pig in her pen. No matter how many different latches the farmer put on the gate, the pig always seemed to figure them out. She would open the latch and escape into the fields. But the farmer was tricky, too. He made a latch that took two steps. To open it, the pig would need to press down a ring and also lift up a hook.

While the pig watched, the farmer put the latch on the gate. He tested it a few times. Then the farmer was curious to see what the pig would do. He decided to hide and watch her. When the farmer was out of her sight, the pig made her move. The farmer said that she opened the latch in thirty seconds. Then she trotted happily into the field.

Scientists think that pigs are in the top-ten list of the world's smartest animals. They communicate with each other using twenty to thirty different sounds.

"Okay, okay," you say. "So pigs are no dummies. But they smell bad! Plus, they roll around in the mud. Yuck!"

You're right about the mud. It's a pretty messy habit. But pigs have a good reason for rolling around in the muck. Pigs don't have sweat glands. Sweating keeps many animals cool. So on hot days, mud helps pigs cool down. It also protects their skin from bugs. The mud even acts as a sunscreen. Pigs can get sunburned, just like people.

Also, pigs themselves don't smell bad. The pigpens where they live can stink, *if* they get too dirty. But that's true of all animals—people, too! (Hmmm. Is it time to clean your room?)

From *Building Character with True Stories from Nature* by Barbara A. Lewis, copyright © 2012. Free Spirit Publishing Inc., Minneapolis, MN; 800-735-7323; www.freespirit.com. This page may be reproduced for use within an individual classroom. For all other uses, contact www.freespirit.com/company/permissions.cfm.

Not all pigs live in pens. Some are pets and live with people inside their homes. LuLu, a potbellied pig, was a pet. She lived with a woman named Jo Ann. And LuLu showed that she was good at sizing up a problem. One day LuLu and Jo Ann were relaxing in Jo Ann's home in the north woods of Pennsylvania. Suddenly Jo Ann had a heart attack. She fell to the floor. Jo Ann was alone, except for her dog and LuLu. She was very scared.

The family dog didn't know what to do other than bark. But LuLu heard Jo Ann's cries. She shuffled over and sniffed out the situation. Then she took action. She crashed her 150-pound body right through the pet door of Jo Ann's home. She cut her tummy on the door's sharp edges. But she didn't stop. She charged out into the fenced-in yard. LuLu hardly ever set hoof outside the yard's gate. Sometimes she had taken walks on a leash. But on this day, she managed to push open the gate all by herself.

LuLu ran to a nearby road and laid down in front of the oncoming cars. Drivers swerved and honked, but LuLu didn't run away. Finally, a young man stopped. He followed LuLu to Jo Ann. Then he called an ambulance and saved Jo Ann's life.

LuLu's courage made her famous. She soon became the best-known pig in Pennsylvania and beyond. Reporters wrote stories about her. They took her picture. But LuLu didn't seem to care about fame. Her favorite reward? A gooey, jelly-filled doughnut.

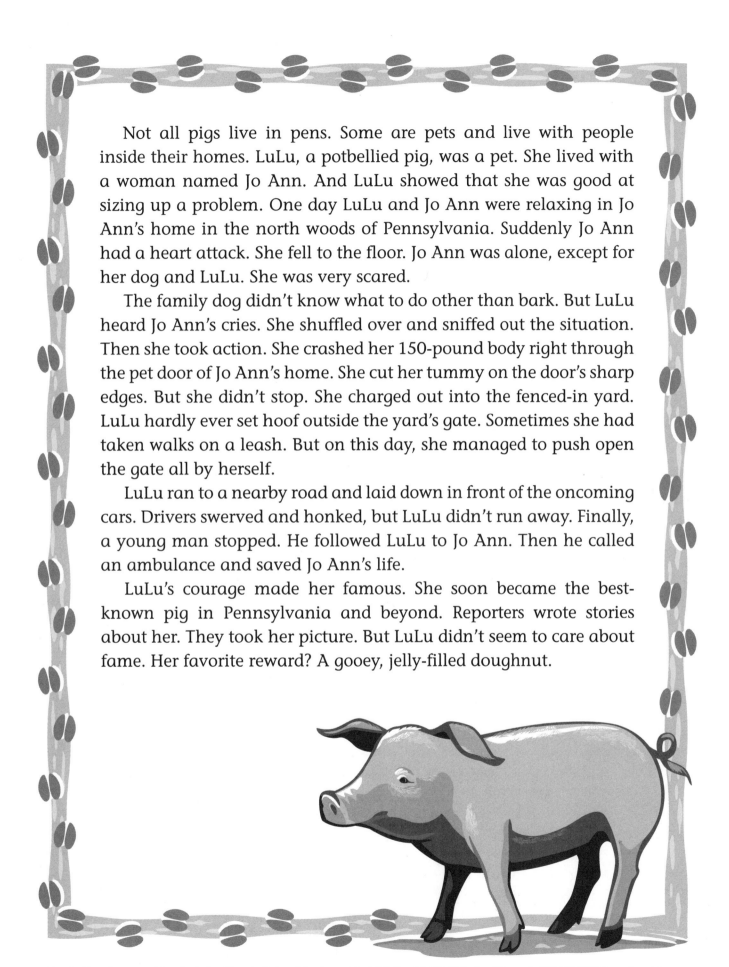

From *Building Character with True Stories from Nature* by Barbara A. Lewis, copyright © 2012. Free Spirit Publishing Inc., Minneapolis, MN; 800-735-7323; www.freespirit.com. This page may be reproduced for use within an individual classroom. For all other uses, contact www.freespirit.com/company/permissions.cfm.

Talk It Over

Use these questions to guide your students in considering analogies between characteristics of pigs and acceptance, courage, and other character traits and behaviors in people.

LuLu showed courage when she left her yard to help her owner. People also show courage by going outside of their comfort zones. What are some examples of people doing something courageous?

- It takes courage to stick up for someone who is being bullied.

- You show courage if you learn that someone in your class is cheating on tests and you report it to your teacher. Other people might make fun of you, but you'll know you did the right thing by telling the truth.

- Many people show courage in times of danger. Firefighters, soldiers, and police officers all risk their lives to protect others. So do people who help others during an emergency or another scary situation, even when it isn't their job.

- Trying something new can take courage. For example, it requires courage to start at a new school, audition for a talent show, try out for a team, or invite a new student to your home.

- We don't all need courage for the same things. Speaking in front of a group is easy for some people and takes courage for others.

Even though many people don't think of pigs as smart, scientists say pigs are very bright. People also think pigs smell bad, but that's not true. Can you compare these false ideas to how people might make false judgments about each other?

- If you get false information about someone, you might make the wrong judgments about him or her. It's best to make a decision for yourself based on what you know for sure is true, rather than what you've only heard from other people.

- Sometimes we can develop prejudices about other people unless we get to know them individually and personally.

- All people deserve respect, regardless of their beliefs, lifestyles, cultures, appearances, or abilities.

- Rumors spread quickly, even (or especially) when they are not true. These rumors can hurt feelings and damage relationships.

- Sometimes false judgments can lead to hatred or violence. *Note:* If desired, you can share the following information with students and talk about it with them: During World War II, the Nazis made untrue statements about Jewish people and other minorities. For example, they said that they were unclean. The Nazis tried to use these false accusations as justification for persecuting and killing many people.

Pigs don't roll around in the mud because they want to be messy. They do this because it keeps them cool and protects their skin from the sun. Can you think of ways that people can protect themselves from things that are uncomfortable, scary, or dangerous?

- Sometimes people who are shy protect themselves from embarrassment or discomfort by being very quiet. They might seem unfriendly, but they are probably just nervous.

- It's important to protect yourself from danger, even if it's not the popular decision. For example, if other kids from school want you to come with them to steal candy from the neighborhood store, you might be worried that they'll laugh at you if you don't agree to go along. But you'll be safer and feel better about yourself if you say no.

Pigs don't naturally smell bad. But when they live in dirty conditions—sometimes because the person who cares for them doesn't keep the pen clean—some people think the pigs themselves are dirty. Can you think of analogies between this idea and human behavior?

- It's risky to judge people based on where they come from or what they look like.

- Pigs in a dirty pen are in a bad situation that they cannot change by themselves. Sometimes people can get into bad situations, too. If you ever need help getting out of a situation, don't be afraid to talk to someone you trust about what's going on.

Pigs show intelligence and problem-solving skills. They have even figured out how to open gates that have complicated latches. How can you compare this to human behavior?

- Pigs can't research problems, but they do have instincts that help them think about what to do. People solve problems by researching their options and looking at different solutions. This research can give people insights and information that help them find the solutions to their problems.

- Sometimes you might face a problem that seems too difficult or complicated to solve. But if you look at each piece of the problem separately, you might be able to figure out answers. Some problems have to be solved in several different steps, just as the pig in Australia had to learn to take two steps to open the latch on the gate.

Pig Facts

Some experts think pigs can solve problems as well as a three-year-old child.

Wild boars are the ancestors of today's domesticated pig. Many kinds of wild pigs still exist.

Pigs have a great sense of smell. They've been trained to sniff out targets from truffles to bombs.

Activities

Activity 1: The Courage Box

Materials
Courage Box handout (on CD-ROM)
Box with lid
Scissors
Pencil
String

Preparation
Make a class Courage Box. Cut a hole in the top of a shoebox or other lidded box, and attach a pencil to the box with string. Print several copies of the Courage Box handout and cut them in half. Place the box and a stack of Courage Box slips somewhere in your classroom.

Directions
Show kids the Courage Box and one of the slips as an example. Invite students to watch for acts of courage among their classmates and other people in their lives. Remind kids that courageous acts aren't always big or showy. Sometimes it takes courage to say hello to a new student, to try out for a play or a sports team, or to speak up for another person.

Explain to the group that when they notice other people showing courage, they can secretly fill out Courage Box slips and put them in the box. Then, depending on how quickly your Courage Box fills up, you can choose a slip once a week or once a month and read it aloud to the class. Invite students to talk about the story, what happened, and how the person showed courage.

Activity 2: Saying Thanks

Materials
Notebook paper or construction paper
Pencils, crayons, and/or markers

Directions
Invite kids to write thank-you notes for gifts of caring, rather than for gifts of physical things. Ask students to think of people who have stood up for them, taken a chance for them, or said nice things to them.

Then ask kids to write thank-you notes or cards to these people. They might be parents, friends, teachers, school principals, or others. Guide kids to include the following in their notes:

- a description of what the other person did
- an explanation of how this kind or caring action affected the note writer
- a "thank you" and the note writer's name

Allow kids to decorate their notes, if desired. Then encourage them to deliver these notes. Afterward, ask them how it felt to say thanks. What was it like to think of caring as a gift? Do they think people expect thanks for these kinds of acts?

Activity 3: Radioactive Slime!

Materials
2 bowls or measuring cups
Hot water
Borax
School glue gel (4 oz.)
Food coloring (yellow, green, or both)
Optional: Yellow highlighter pen
Optional: Plastic bag

Preparation
Before beginning this activity with your group, create slime ahead of time with a few simple ingredients and the following procedure:

- Measure out ½ cup of hot water in a bowl or measuring cup. Little by little, stir borax into the water. Continue adding and stirring until the borax stops dissolving.

- Measure out 1 cup of hot water in a second, larger bowl or measuring cup. Stir 4 ounces of glue gel into the water. Add a few drops of food coloring to the glue mixture. You can use just a couple of drops of yellow food coloring, or two drops of yellow and one drop of green. (A yellow highlighter pen makes the best fluorescent coloring. Break it open and let it bleed into the mixture.)

- Mix ⅓ cup of the borax solution with 1 cup of the glue solution. When they combine you'll create a gooey, slimy mixture. The food coloring will make it look slightly glowy and radioactive. *Note:* When you mix the glue and borax solutions together, a chemical change happens in the glue. It causes the glue to stick to you less and to stick to itself more.

- If you don't plan to use the slime for a while, you can store it in a sealed plastic bag to keep it from drying out.

Directions
When you show the slime to your group, tell them that you have a great new product. It's a special glue that might even be used to hold together cars, planes, and rockets. The only trouble is that it's slightly radioactive. Explain that this means that if you touch it, you could get sick. (Depending on your group, you can elaborate on this idea as much or as little as desired.)

Variation: To reinforce the idea of the "radioactive" slime as dangerous, you could wear plastic gloves and safety glasses while you show your group the slime.

Invite a volunteer to touch the slime—but only briefly. You may or may not get any volunteers! If you do, urge them to wash their hands right away after touching the slime.

Carry this deception as far as you feel is appropriate for your group. Then let kids in on your secret. Tell them that, instead of being dangerous, the ingredients in the slime are actually harmless and even useful. Once kids have learned the truth, invite them to share how they felt about the slime before, and how they feel now. Use this as a starting point to talk about how an untruth or a misconception can sometimes lead people to shrink away from something or someone. Encourage kids to consider analogies to prejudice and discrimination, which often begin with false impressions and inaccurate information.

Lesson 21
Quaking Aspen Trees

Character Key Words
Cooperation • Inner Strength • Adaptability • Integrity • Self-Control

Students will
- learn interesting facts about the quaking aspen tree, including about a huge, inter-connected grove of aspen called Pando, and make analogies to human character traits
- draw an analogy between the aspen's connected roots and cooperation and adaptability among people
- compare the trembling leaves of aspen trees to people who may not be physically strong but who have self-control, integrity, and inner strength

Overview
Standing on the rolling hills of Utah's Fishlake National Forest is a colony of more than 45,000 aspen trees, their delicate leaves fluttering in the wind. The colony's massive root system dates back an estimated 80,000 years. Together, this huge aspen grove—known by names such as Pando and the Trembling Giant—is believed to be among the largest and oldest living organisms on the planet.

With their prolific growth and great longevity, aspen trees are models of survival and adaptability. They derive much of their success from the interconnectedness of their roots, all of which belong to a single plant. This underground root system continues to send up new shoots even as old ones die. The trees themselves are slender and delicate. But together, they have strength. Similarly, people gain strength from cooperation, self-control, and integrity, whether in classrooms, families, or communities. These traits can make people stronger as a group than they would be as individuals.

Story
Quaking Aspen Trees

Quaking Aspen Trees

It is one of the world's largest living things. Experts think it weighs more than 13 million pounds. (No one knows for sure. There's no scale big enough to weigh it!) Any guesses? It's not a massive polar bear. It's not a blue whale. It's not a giant redwood. But it *is* a tree.

It's called Pando. Pando is a grove of quaking aspen trees in Fishlake National Forest in Utah. It covers more than 100 acres and has about 47,000 aspen tree trunks. Pando lives up to its name. The word *pando* means "I spread" in Latin. Sometimes people also call Pando the Trembling Giant. When the wind blows, it looks like the whole forest is trembling. Delicate aspen leaves flutter in the breeze. They make a beautiful rustling sound. In the fall the leaves turn bright yellow. They float to the ground like golden coins.

How can a tree grow to be one of the world's largest living things? Aspen trees grow very fast. But that isn't the answer. Pando's real secret? Its thousands of trunks may look separate. But they all belong to one big plant. A huge underground root system connects them. Each trunk is like a branch on a giant tree. Scientists think this root system is at least 80,000 years old. That makes it one of the world's *oldest* living things, too.

These ancient roots keep Pando alive. Sometimes windstorms or wildfires rip through the forest. Individual aspen trunks die. Yet below the surface, the roots survive. Soon they start sending up new shoots. They bring hope that the forest will live on.

From *Building Character with True Stories from Nature* by Barbara A. Lewis, copyright © 2012. Free Spirit Publishing Inc., Minneapolis, MN; 800-735-7323; www.freespirit.com. This page may be reproduced for use within an individual classroom. For all other uses, contact www.freespirit.com/company/permissions.cfm.

But now Pando is in trouble. Many branches are dying. And not many new ones are growing.

Maybe the huge plant is just getting old. Another problem could be the trees' neighbors. Forest animals like deer and elk eat the tree's young shoots. Many new branches never get a chance to grow tall. Once wolves roamed the forest. They kept down the number of deer and elk. But the area has few wolves now. Other animals gnaw on the aspens' white bark. Beetles and other insects sometimes harm the trees.

Pando has adapted to changes and challenges many times during its long, long life. Can Pando save itself this time? Or does it need help? No one wants this natural wonder to fade away. So people are thinking about how to rescue Pando. How do *you* think we could help Pando?

From *Building Character with True Stories from Nature* by Barbara A. Lewis, copyright © 2012. Free Spirit Publishing Inc., Minneapolis, MN; 800-735-7323; www.freespirit.com. This page may be reproduced for use within an individual classroom. For all other uses, contact www.freespirit.com/company/permissions.cfm.

Talk It Over

Use these questions to guide your students in considering analogies between quaking aspen trees and cooperation, inner strength, and other character traits and behaviors in people.

The word *pando* means "I spread" in Latin. What connections can you draw between the spread of aspen trees across the hillsides and things that can spread among people?

- Rumors and name-calling can spread rapidly, and they can be very hurtful. The sooner they're stopped, the better.

- Friendliness and happiness can spread quickly, too. If you're kind to people, they may pass along that kindness to others.

- Diseases and viruses can spread quickly if people are not careful.

Aspen trees have delicate leaves that tremble in the breeze. But Pando is strong. Can you compare the aspen tree's trembling leaves to human traits?

- Strength comes in many forms. Physical strength is only one. Self-control, integrity, and adaptability are all forms of inner strength.

- Everyone is afraid of something. Even someone who seems fearless probably worries about things such as doing well in school, playing sports, developing a talent, or gaining friends.

- A person's size does not determine how strong, brave, or kind he or she is.

- Fear itself is not weakness. For example, sometimes fear helps us stay safe. If you are in a situation or place that is causing you to feel scared, get away or get help.

Aspen trees face threats such as animals and insects that eat or damage the bark. Sometimes the trees rot inside. Can you make an analogy to habits and experiences that people have?

- People can destroy their happiness and sense of peace by being filled with anger, hatred, or negative thoughts. They can "rot" inside.

- Not eating nutritious foods, exercising regularly, or practicing healthful habits can cause you to be sick inside, physically and mentally.

- If you use harmful substances—such as drugs, alcohol, or cigarettes—you can become sick or addicted. It's important to have self-control to avoid these temptations.

The secret behind Pando's long life is the underground root system connecting all its trunks. How does this connectedness relate to people and their communities?

- A strong root system is like a family. When family members support, help, and respect each other, the family is stronger as a whole.

- If you are anchored by good character traits, you will be stronger when you face challenges in life. You can also share your strength with others by helping them face challenges.

- When families, friends, classes, teams, and communities agree on shared goals, they reach them more easily. They help each other work toward these goals.

- Having integrity means that your actions are deeply connected with your values and beliefs. You don't change your behavior to please others. You have inner strength. You are trustworthy, consistent, and dependable.

The Pando aspen grove has adapted to many changes over the years. It may be able to rescue itself again, or it might need help. Can you compare this adaptability to the behavior of people?

- When you learn that you are doing something wrong, you need to be able to adapt. You can learn a new way to behave or a different way to approach a challenge.

- Times change. The world changes. Lives change. People often need to adapt to new conditions, such as moving to a new school, having new family members, and so on.

- Anytime you have a problem, you'll have more success solving the problem if you can be flexible and adaptable. Coping with change can be hard, but it's a good ability to have.

- Adaptability is a helpful and positive skill to have. But everyone needs help sometimes, too. Knowing when to ask others for help is also a good skill.

Quaking Aspen Facts

Several quaking aspen groves often grow in the same area. You can tell which trunks are in the same family by looking for similarities such as the shape of their trunks.

Quaking aspen trees grow in all but thirteen of the U.S. states and in all the provinces of Canada.

Several different Native American tribes have traditionally used aspen bark to treat various injuries and sicknesses.

Activities

Activity 1: The Cooperation Tree

Materials

Cooperation Tree handout (on CD-ROM)
Optional: Aspen Leaf handout (on CD-ROM)
Colored pencils
Optional: Chart paper or a bulletin board
Optional: Yarn or construction paper
Optional: Kid-safe scissors

Directions

Create a list of guidelines, goals, and rules for your class. Discuss with your group the kinds of rules that would help your classroom become an even better place to learn. Focus the conversation on cooperation, helpfulness, and mutual support and respect. For example, "Our classroom is a better place for learning when everyone listens." As kids brainstorm, write down their ideas on the board.

Together, choose six to ten rules for your class to focus on. Pass out copies of the Cooperation Tree handout and have kids fill in the leaves with the guidelines and rules your group has chosen. Kids can also decorate the leaves or color them if they like.

Variation: Create a large Cooperation Tree in your space. On chart paper or a bulletin board, draw an outline of a bare tree or create one out of yarn or construction paper. Pass out copies of the Aspen Leaf handout and ask kids to decorate the leaves, write their names on them, and cut them out. Have some kids write the rules you've chosen on leaves, or write these yourself. Then attach all the leaves to the "tree."

Activity 2: Standing Strong

Materials

None

Directions

Have kids stand with their eyes closed and their arms up in the air. Tell them to pretend that they are aspens in the Pando grove, and their fingers are their leaves. Next, make statements that address and test integrity. Some should be positive, and some negative. For example, *I have stood up for someone who was being bullied.* Or, *Sometimes I have told lies.* Tell kids to wiggle their fingers like Pando's trembling leaves if the statement is true for them. If the statement does not apply to them, they should hold their hands still. Remind them that no one else can see how they answer, and assure them that you won't tell anyone, either.

After most kids have wiggled their fingers a few times, ask kids to open their eyes and sit in a circle. Without singling anyone out, ask kids to think and talk about whether they would have felt afraid or embarrassed to answer honestly if their classmates could see them. Discuss the idea that integrity can be described as doing what you know is right, even if no one else sees or knows about it.

Pick a topic from one of the statements you made during the activity, such as honesty, and focus on this idea for a while. Ask kids if they think it would be easier to tell the truth if they knew the people around them were all truthful, too. Discuss the way it can be easier to stick to our values when the people around us support our positive character traits and behaviors. Having support from the outside can strengthen our integrity. But we can also draw strength from ourselves, like Pando draws strength from its roots, by staying connected to our own values and beliefs, even when other people might disagree or make fun of us for doing so.

Activity 3: Connecting the Circuit

Materials
Flashlight bulb or small globe bulb
Size D battery
8–12 inches of copper wire
Wire cutters or scissors
Electrical or duct tape

Preparation
Make a simple circuit. First, cut the wire in half. Use scissors to scrape off about 1 inch of the plastic insulation at each end of both wires. Cut two small pieces of tape. Tape the end of one wire to the bottom, or negative, terminal of the battery. Tape one end of the other wire to the top, or positive, terminal of the battery.

Test your circuit. Touch the end of the negative-terminal wire to the threading around the light bulb's base. (This is one of the bulb's terminals.) Finally, to complete the circuit, touch the other wire (connected to the battery's positive terminal) to the foot of the lightbulb. The light should come on.

Directions
Begin this demonstration with the wires attached to the battery but not the bulb. Show kids that when you connect all parts of the circuit by touching the wires to the right points on the bulb, the light comes on. Electricity is flowing through the wires between the battery and the bulb. But if any part of the circuit is disconnected, the circuit is broken. The light goes out. Invite volunteers to try connecting and breaking the circuit for themselves.

Talk with the group about how these ideas apply to people. For example, when everyone in a family, classroom, or other group cooperates and works together, it's like the circuit is connected. Sometimes you have to adapt and use self-control to follow group goals. While it's not always easy to do this, it helps things go more smoothly. But if some people are not cooperating or doing their share of the work, it can break the "circuit" by disrupting the group.

Similarly, every person has his or her own set of values and beliefs. When we act according to those beliefs, we show integrity. We feel whole, as though our internal circuit is connected. But when we do things that go against our positive values, it's like we're breaking the circuit. We may feel uncomfortable or sad. Ask kids to talk about these ideas. When have they showed integrity and kept the circuit connected? How does it feel? Why is it hard to do this sometimes?

Lesson 22
Squirrels

Character Key Words
Hard Work • Planning and Preparation • Curiosity • Conservation

Students will
- learn about squirrels and some of their characteristics, including their hardworking nature and their behavior of gathering and storing food
- analyze the value of being prepared for the future, and discuss the idea that even when people try to prepare, they may need help
- create an analogy between the squirrel's curiosity and people's desire to learn
- connect the squirrel's dependence on nature's abundance to the way people also depend on nature to support life

Overview
People seem either to love squirrels or loathe them. Squirrels' industry and energy set a great example. But their curiosity and boldness can sometimes cause headaches for gardeners, homeowners, and bird watchers. You will probably find that many of your students have their own squirrel stories to tell, and you can use their anecdotes to lay the groundwork for this lesson. The story will spark discussions about character and serve as a jumping-off point for activities that reinforce positive traits such as hard work, curiosity, and preparation.

The squirrel's story and habits also connect to conservation. Gray squirrels bury thousands of nuts in a season. Their lives depend in large part upon nature's plenty. And they give back to the planet's health. When they can't find or forget some of their hidden caches of food, some of the buried nuts may grow into trees, helping replenish and maintain forests. Squirrels serve as a reminder that people need to respect nature and help preserve its diversity.

Story
Spirited Squirrels

Spirited Squirrels

Have you ever seen a squirrel leaping from one tree branch to another? Squirrels sail through the air like tiny acrobats. They have strong legs, and they are great jumpers. Squirrels are good runners, too. They usually run about 8 to 10 miles per hour. But red and gray squirrels have been clocked at 20 miles per hour. They can dash especially fast if they're being chased by hawks or other predators.

What if a squirrel slips off a high branch? Some squirrels have survived long falls from tall trees. They use their tails as fluffy parachutes. This slows them down as they fall. But even nimble squirrels can get hurt if they fall too far.

Squirrels are a type of rodent. They build different kinds of nests. If you see a big clump of leaves piled up in a tree, it might be a squirrel nest. Other times, squirrels nest inside holes in trees. Ground squirrels dig burrows in the ground. Squirrels use twigs, bark, and leaves to build their nests. They also like to make them soft and comfy. They gather string, feathers, and pet hair. They might even pull the stuffing right out of outdoor chair cushions!

And sometimes, tricky squirrels move in with humans. When the weather gets cold, some squirrels look for shelter in attics or walls. If you hear the sound of little claws tapping in the ceiling, you might have a squirrel roommate.

Squirrels always seem to be hungry. Gutsy gray squirrels sometimes walk right up to campers, hikers, and tourists. Has a squirrel ever begged you for your sandwich? He might even have rested his paws on your foot or leg. But watch out. Squirrels' teeth and claws are sharp. So be very careful if you reach out your hand to feed a squirrel. He could mistake your finger for a tasty peanut.

From *Building Character with True Stories from Nature* by Barbara A. Lewis, copyright © 2012. Free Spirit Publishing Inc., Minneapolis, MN; 800-735-7323; www.freespirit.com. This page may be reproduced for use within an individual classroom. For all other uses, contact www.freespirit.com/company/permissions.cfm.

Squirrels love to eat nuts. They also gobble up seeds, fruits, and twigs. They eat flower buds, pinecones, and mushrooms. If you let them, they'll eat your leftover sandwich, too. In fact, squirrels will try just about anything. In the summer and fall, they spend lots of time busily gathering food. They work hard to store food for the winter. They bury nuts and other food in hundreds of different spots. That's a lot to remember when winter comes. Scientists have learned that gray squirrels can't always find some of their stashed food. That's bad news for the squirrel. But it can be good for the planet. Some of the nuts that squirrels forget or lose can grow into trees.

Squirrels can be sneaky with their food, too. If a squirrel notices that someone is watching, he may pretend to bury a nut. But he really keeps it in his cheek. Then he moves out of sight and buries it somewhere else. Gotcha!

In addition to being clever, squirrels are curious and bold. Some people like squirrels a lot. It can be fun and entertaining to watch them romp and play. They scold you with their chattering as they scamper and climb.

But some people think these animals are pests. Gardeners complain that squirrels run off with their tomatoes. Birdwatchers who put out seed for songbirds get frustrated when squirrels eat some of it. People have tried to invent "squirrel-proof" feeders, but squirrels usually figure them out. A hungry squirrel rarely gives up!

From *Building Character with True Stories from Nature* by Barbara A. Lewis, copyright © 2012. Free Spirit Publishing Inc., Minneapolis, MN; 800-735-7323; www.freespirit.com.
This page may be reproduced for use within an individual classroom. For all other uses, contact www.freespirit.com/company/permissions.cfm.

Talk It Over

Use these questions to guide your students in considering analogies between squirrels and curiosity, preparation, and other character traits and behaviors in people.

Squirrels work very hard to make their nests and to gather and store food for the winter. Can you compare this habit to a human behavior?

- Family members often work hard to care for and support each other.

- Kids work hard, too. They can help with chores at home and in the classroom. When everyone pitches in, tasks get done more quickly and the work goes more smoothly.

- Preparing for the future isn't always easy, but it's important. For example, it's a good idea to save money when you can, so that you have enough later on.

- Planning and preparing for the future doesn't always mean saving money, food, or other supplies. It can mean studying hard and making other good decisions.

- Working to reach a goal can be difficult or tiring, but it's also rewarding. And even when we don't meet our goal, we can learn from our experience.

Squirrels bury so many nuts each season that they lose track of some of them. But that's not all bad. Some of these nuts grow into trees, which helps restore forests. Can you think of ways that you can help the environment, too?

- You can use less paper, water, and electricity every day. You can also recycle paper, cans, plastic, and other materials from your classroom, lunchroom, and home.

- You can help animals by feeding them and caring for them. For example, you could volunteer at local animal shelters, or put out nuts and seeds for squirrels and birds in the winter.

- You can help animals that are endangered. You could raise money for organizations that help protect threatened animals, or you could learn about these animals and share that information with other people. Knowing more about a problem often inspires people to take action.

- You can help plant trees. Trees help clean the air, provide homes for animals, and prevent erosion.

- You can be sure never to litter. You can also help clean up trash in rivers, lakes, and other areas.

Squirrels are very good at remembering where they stored nuts and other food, but it can still be hard for them to keep track of all their hundreds of storage spots. Sometimes people have trouble remembering things, too. How can we help ourselves remember and prepare for what we need to do?

- Write down homework assignments in a binder or notebook each day. Read your list when you get home to remind yourself of what you need to do.

- Before you leave for school in the morning, double-check that you have everything you need for the day.

- If there are tasks that are your responsibility at home, make a list of them each day or each week.

- If you're working on a big paper, dance routine, or other project, sometimes it can feel overwhelming at first. You can try breaking down the big project into smaller steps. Then you can check off each step as you get it done and move on to the next one.

Squirrels are curious and persistent. They can get into chimneys, attics, walls, and even cars. Their curiosity also leads them to taste just about any sort of food they find. Can you compare this to people who are curious? Is curiosity positive, negative, or both? How so?

- Curiosity can often lead to discovery. When you're curious about something, your brain is active and learning.

- Curiosity has inspired people to discover cures for diseases, create inventions, and develop new ideas that change the world.

- Curiosity can be dangerous if it leads you to practice harmful habits or get involved in risky situations. Be careful that your curiosity doesn't cause you to go against your values or the character traits you know are positive.

Squirrel Facts

Squirrels live on every continent except Australia and Antarctica. There are more than 275 different species of squirrels, which are a type of rodent.

Flying squirrels don't really fly. They leap and glide. Some species can glide as far as 150 to 200 feet. As they glide, flying squirrels can even turn and steer to avoid branches.

In addition to using their tails for balance, squirrels also use them to communicate.

Activities

Activity 1: Squirrel Snacks

Materials

Wooden boxes, tin cans, or other containers
Nuts and seeds

Directions

Even with all their preparation, sometimes squirrels don't have enough food to last them through the winter. Your class can help squirrels, birds, chipmunks, and other animals by making and setting out wildlife feeders. In the course of this activity, your group can also talk about the importance of helping those in need.

You can find instructions for making a variety of simple wildlife feeders at the following website: www.birdsandblooms.com/Backyard-Projects/Bird-Feeders. Work together as a class to make and decorate the feeder (or more than one feeder, if you like). Finally, fill the feeder with seeds, nuts, or other wildlife-friendly food, and hang it up. If possible, place it where you can see it from your classroom. If that's not an option, once a day or so, take kids to a spot where they can see the feeder. Kids will love watching animals visit the feeder to eat.

Talk with kids about this experience. How did it feel to help some of the animals in your neighborhood? Would they like to take this action at home, too? What are other ways they could help local wildlife? Discuss the idea that service does not have to be dramatic or have a wide scope to be important and helpful. Small actions can make a big difference, too.

Note: Be sure to remind your group that squirrels, songbirds, chipmunks, and other wild animals are not pets. They can act unpredictably. It's better for wild animals and for us if we keep a safe distance from each other.

Activity 2: Planting Curiosity

Materials

Planting Curiosity handout (on CD-ROM)

Directions

Kids are curious about many things, and curiosity can stimulate the brain and support learning. But kids don't always follow up these interests by looking into them more deeply. This activity encourages them to choose topics of curiosity and pursue them in a more focused and intentional way.

Pass out copies of the Planting Curiosity handout. Invite kids to brainstorm three things that they're curious about and about which they'd like to learn more. *Note:* If helpful, encourage them to phrase their ideas as questions. For example, "How do flying squirrels glide?" Or, "What more can I learn about Mars?"

Ask kids to write one curiosity starting point on each buried acorn, and then to choose one of these three ideas to serve as the basis for a research project. Tell them that a little seed of curiosity can be the start of something big. Just as squirrels help forests thrive by "planting" nuts, kids can use their curiosity questions to expand their knowledge and interests.

If desired, send notes home with kids to let families know about the project and encouraging them to help kids search for information about their topics. Set a due date for the research, and ask kids to report their findings to the class. But also remind them that this due date doesn't have to be the end of their exploration. It could be just the beginning. Maybe as kids answered some questions, they also found new ones to wonder about. Curiosity can grow and grow.

Activity 3: A Plan to Help Out with Hunger

Materials

Various

Directions

Squirrels gather as much food as they can, but sometimes they still go hungry during a long winter. When that happens, they need help. Talk with kids about how people around the world also struggle with hunger, and explain that they need help, too. Discuss the problem of hunger in faraway places and also in your own community. Then brainstorm a list of ways that your group can help fight hunger, close to home and beyond. Ideas could include holding a fund-raiser and sending the funds to an international organization fighting global hunger; volunteering at a food shelf; donating canned goods to a local shelter; or planting a community garden to help grow food for the hungry.

Choose one idea to put into action. Before getting started, talk with kids about the importance of planning and preparation in carrying out your project. As a group, create a plan with specific steps and goals. This project could extend over weeks or even months, depending on your group's age, interests, and resources. Whatever service you decide to undertake, create a detailed plan and recruit help from parents or other volunteers as needed. When you've completed your project, ask each student to write a short essay, story, or poem about the experience, or to draw a picture showing part of the action your group took. If desired, you could compile these pieces into a booklet that kids can share with family and friends.

Lesson 23
Turkeys

Character Key Words
Fairness and Equality • Respect • Tolerance and Acceptance • Responsibility • Citizenship

Students will
- learn interesting facts about turkeys, such as differences between farm turkeys and wild turkeys, and draw comparisons to human character traits
- compare false stereotypes about turkeys to the way people sometimes stereotype each other, and the need to treat others with fairness, tolerance, and acceptance
- draw an analogy between the lack of respect that many people show for turkeys to people who display a lack of respect for those who are different from them
- examine the social habits of turkeys and their responsible care of their young, and compare these attributes to people who take civic responsibility to care for others

Overview
The word *turkey* refers to a species of birds, but it is also sometimes used as an insult. Many people believe that turkeys are unintelligent, slow, and awkward. In fact, turkeys are quite bright. And while overfed farm turkeys are flightless and may live in very unpleasant conditions, wild turkeys are agile fliers and have interesting social habits and family structures.

These contrasts will provide you and your students with excellent starting points for exploring character traits and behaviors including fairness, respect, and acceptance. Turkeys share responsibilities in caring for their young and live in social groups. Exploring these traits can provide your group with opportunities to discuss the importance of responsibility and citizenship.

Story
Terrific Turkeys

Terrific Turkeys

"How can I soar with the eagles when I'm surrounded by turkeys?"

"What a turkey!"

"Oh, boy. I feel as dumb as a turkey."

Have you ever heard insults like these? It seems like turkeys get a bad rap. Even the thesaurus isn't very nice to them. *Birdbrain. Buffoon. Simpleton. Twerp.* These are just a few of the synonyms it gives for *turkey.*

But are turkeys really dumb?

Experts say turkeys are actually smart, social birds. Some of the false ideas people have about turkeys come from the way the birds are raised on farms. Farm turkeys are fed until they weigh twice as much as their wild cousins. These turkeys get too heavy to fly. But they still have the instinct to take flight. They may run and flap their wings hopelessly, never leaving the ground. These turkeys may appear awkward, comical, and not very bright.

In the wild, things are different. Wild turkeys can fly at speeds of 50 miles per hour. That's almost as fast as a car on the highway! And wild turkeys are fast on land, too. They can run up to 25 miles per hour.

Maybe you've heard another story about turkeys. People say the birds look up while it's raining. Then they keep staring until they drown. That doesn't sound too smart, does it? But is it true? Turkeys *do* sometimes stare at the sky, even when it rains. But they aren't cuckoo. A medical condition causes some turkeys to do this. They can't help it. And most experts don't think that turkeys really drown this way.

Some people also think that turkeys aren't very bright because young farm turkeys sometimes starve, even when there's food nearby. How does this happen? In the wild, adult turkeys teach youngsters how to find and eat food. But on many farms, turkeys don't live with their families. Instead, they may be crowded into dark, smelly sheds.

From *Building Character with True Stories from Nature* by Barbara A. Lewis, copyright © 2012. Free Spirit Publishing Inc., Minneapolis, MN; 800-735-7323; www.freespirit.com. This page may be reproduced for use within an individual classroom. For all other uses, contact www.freespirit.com/company/permissions.cfm.

Young turkeys are separated from their parents. They don't learn by watching grown-up turkeys. So sometimes these young birds can't find food and water. They're not dumb. They're just alone and confused.

Wild turkeys are rarely alone. Before a turkey chick even hatches from its egg, it can hear its mother's voice. After hatching, the baby turkey can walk and leave the nest almost right away. But chicks stay with the flock. Young turkeys sleep on the ground, snuggled under their mothers' wings. Later they fly to roost on low tree branches. Female turkeys, called hens, share the job of caring for chicks and showing them how to find food.

Sometimes, as a young turkey scampers around and hunts bugs, he might lose track of where his mother is. Then the young turkey raises his head high and calls out loudly. He listens for his mother's answer. They call until they find each other. Sometimes the whole flock may stop until mother and baby reunite.

As youngsters grow up, they stay in groups. Wild turkeys are very social. They feel safest when they're with other turkeys. During summer and fall, turkey hens that have chicks stick together. Older hens flock with each other. Older male gobblers hang out together, too, while spirited, spunky young males form noisy groups of their own.

It seems like smart, social turkeys deserve more respect than people usually give them. And in the United States, people have an extra reason to care about turkeys. In the 1600s, Native Americans introduced turkeys to pilgrims in North America. Those were hard times for the new settlers. Eating turkeys helped people survive. Now, the turkey is a traditional Thanksgiving symbol of family, love, and togetherness.

From *Building Character with True Stories from Nature* by Barbara A. Lewis, copyright © 2012. Free Spirit Publishing Inc., Minneapolis, MN; 800-735-7323; www.freespirit.com. This page may be reproduced for use within an individual classroom. For all other uses, contact www.freespirit.com/company/permissions.cfm.

Talk It Over

Use these questions to guide your students in considering analogies between turkeys and respect, fairness, and other character traits and behaviors in people.

Sometimes people use the word *turkey* as an insult. But turkeys are smart, social birds. What analogies can you draw between this false labeling of turkeys and ways that people might treat others?

- Name-calling is hurtful and unkind. If it happens over and over again, it can be a form of bullying. Bullying is never okay. If you are being bullied or you know someone who is, tell a grown-up.

- If someone calls you a turkey, it doesn't make you a turkey—anymore than calling you a toad makes you a toad. It's hard to ignore mean and hurtful words. But if you can refuse to believe unkind things that someone says about you, you will get stronger and more confident over time.

- Rumors can spread faster than wildfire. If a lot of people believe a rumor, someone may end up with an unfairly charred reputation. It's best not to start or spread rumors.

- Sometimes turkeys on farms flap their wings awkwardly in an instinctive attempt to fly. Similarly, sometimes people look unsure or awkward as they work toward difficult goals. But we shouldn't make fun of these people. It takes courage to try hard and aim for a big goal. We all make mistakes and we all look silly sometimes. But everyone deserves respect.

Turkeys are associated with negative stereotypes that are mostly untrue. On the flip side, sometimes people such as athletes and movie stars are associated with positive stereotypes. These aren't always true, either. What are some of the risks of stereotyping or labeling people?

- Sometimes idolizing a person can lead to disappointment if you find out that your hero is not what he or she appears to be.

- A negative stereotype of a group of people transfers a bad reputation to everyone involved. It's important to have respect for every person as an individual. Everyone is different.

- If you stereotype a person and assume that he or she is a certain way, you might miss out on making a good friend or getting to know someone really interesting.

- In very extreme situations, stereotyping and prejudice can lead to viewing an entire culture or group of people as less valuable than others. These negative and destructive ideas can lead to tragedies such as slavery and genocide (the attempt to destroy an entire group of people).

Turkeys have a medical reason for some of their actions, such as staring at the sky. Can you make an analogy to human behavior?

- Some people have trouble walking or speaking. Other people might not hear or see well. Sometimes it can be confusing when we meet someone who has a physical challenge. But it may help to understand that there's a medical reason for a person's behavior. And it's important to be kind and respectful to all people.

- We can't know what challenges people have just by looking at them. Sometimes people may have emotional or mental issues that we can't see. It's important never to make assumptions about others.

People who believe that turkeys are stupid are lacking accurate information. They make unfair assumptions about all turkeys. Do people have unfair ideas about each other, too?

- Sometimes people use stereotypes to justify having false ideas about others. Stereotypes and prejudice are unfair.

- A person might dislike one person who has certain beliefs or a certain lifestyle. Sometimes he or she then transfers that dislike for this single person to all people who share those beliefs or lifestyle. But it isn't fair to lump all people together like that. Every person deserves respect as an individual.

Turkeys are very sociable and like to live in groups. Within these groups, they share some responsibilities. Can you compare this idea to the way people live in communities? How do people share responsibilities and show citizenship?

- People have responsibilities in families to help each other. All members of a family have chores that need to be done. For example, small kids can put away toys. Older brothers and sisters may help take care of their younger siblings.

- Communities, states, and countries have organizations to help people who need homes, food, or other help.

- Within classrooms, students have different responsibilities that help keep the class running smoothly.

- People show responsibility and citizenship by following laws, taking part in the community, and understanding how the government works.

Turkey Facts

A male turkey's distinctive gobbling call can be heard a mile away.

The flap of skin under a turkey's chin is called a wattle. It changes color when the turkey is frightened, aggressive, or sick, or when he is courting a female.

Benjamin Franklin once wrote that he wished the wild turkey would become the national bird of the United States instead of the bald eagle. He described the turkey as "a Bird of Courage."

Activities

Activity 1: Fair and Equal

Materials
None

Directions
Divide kids into two groups based on when their birthdays are. Place all kids with birthdays between January and May in one group and kids with birthdays between June and December in the other. Declare that the kids born between January and May are better students and will have the leadership in the class. Treat them specially for a period of time. For example:

- Seat them together in a certain section of your room.

- Tell them they'll be able to skip one of today's homework assignments.

- Ask them to line up first at lunchtime.

As the day progresses, keep a close eye on kids to see how they're reacting. End the exercise when you feel it's appropriate. Then gather your group in a circle and explain what was going on. Reassure all kids that their birthdays do not determine their character, intelligence, or worth as people. Ask students in both groups to share how this experience made them feel. Discuss what it means to be fair and equal with everyone. Make sure that kids understand that everyone is different and not everyone has the same skills and talents. However, all people should be treated fairly. Brainstorm ways to be fair and equal in your class.

Activity 2: The Respect Report

Materials
None

Directions
Divide your group into pairs of students. Have each pair brainstorm a list of the ways to show respect for different people, groups, and ideas. (For example: classmates, friends, parents, siblings, teachers, a school principal, coaches, laws, the environment.)

Assign one person in each pair to write down their ideas and the other person to report to the big group.

When kids have had some time to work, ask the reporters to stand up and share their lists. Talk about the different ideas and the many ways we can show respect for others. Ask kids why respect is important. How does it feel when people respect us? What about when they show disrespect toward us?

After the discussion, combine all the lists into one big list and create a classroom display of the list.

Variation: To spread the message of respect beyond the classroom, you could send the list home to families in a newsletter. If your class has a website, you could post the list there, as well.

Activity 3: Character Puppets

Materials

Paper sacks (1 per student)
Crayons, markers, colored pencils
Yarn, buttons, colored paper, and other items for
     decorating puppets
School glue

Directions

Ask kids to make puppets out of paper sacks. Divide the class into groups of two to four and ask kids to create and perform short puppet shows acting out situations in which characters show respect to each other. For example, one group could show a student or students being respectful to a teacher by speaking politely and following directions.

Variation: If you've completed the Respect Report activity, ask the same pairs from that activity to base their puppet shows on ideas from the Respect Report.

Activity 4: Links of Citizenship

Materials

Links of Citizenship handout (on CD-ROM)
Kid-safe scissors
Tape
Optional: Colored pencils, markers, crayons

Directions

Turkeys take good care of their young. And within their social groups, they share responsibilities. Talk with kids about how this relates to ideas of citizenship and how people take care of each other and of their communities, too. For example, not littering is one way to be a good citizen. As a group, brainstorm acts of good citizenship.

Pass out copies of the Links of Citizenship handout. Have each kid write one way to be a good citizen on his or her link. (It's fine if there are duplicates.) If desired, kids can color or decorate their links. Then ask them to cut them out and help you make a citizenship chain out of all the links. Use tape to secure the links.

Explore the idea that, if everyone is a good citizen, we can build a strong community together. And tell kids that the chain isn't complete yet. Whenever they see someone being a good citizen, they can add another link to the chain. Or, if they have new ideas for acts of good citizenship, they can add those to the chain, too. Hang the chain somewhere in your room and watch it grow and grow.

Lesson 24
Venus Flytraps

Character Key Words
Adaptability • Good Decision-Making • Self-Control

Students will
- learn about the Venus flytrap and some of its characteristics, including the way it traps its prey
- draw comparisons between the Venus flytrap's adaptability and the need for people to adapt to new situations
- create analogies between bugs that get caught by the Venus flytrap and the ways that self-control can protect people from dangerous situations or poor decisions
- consider the way the flytrap catches prey and draw connections to the need for people to have good decision-making skills and to take responsibility for their choices

Overview
Some writers and filmmakers have shown the Venus flytrap as a bloodthirsty monster because of its appetite for spiders and insects. But the Venus flytrap also presents a great opportunity for discussing adaptability. Growing in the nutrient-poor soil of hot, humid bogs, the Venus flytrap developed its insectivorous diet as a way to obtain necessary nitrogen and other nutrients. Kids will be fascinated by this unusual plant and will enjoy making analogies between flytraps—and their prey—and human character traits and behaviors such as self-control and accepting responsibility for the consequences of decisions.

Story
Snappy Venus Flytraps

Snappy Venus Flytraps

Have you ever heard of a movie star that's a plant?

Meet Audrey! She was the main character in a movie called *The Little Shop of Horrors*. She was a gigantic Venus flytrap. Audrey had a big appetite. The monster plant would cry to her owner, "Feed me, Seymour!" And Audrey was picky about what she ate. Her favorite meal? *People*.

The Venus flytrap is a real plant. But don't worry. It's small, not huge. And it doesn't really eat people. It dines on insects and spiders. Still, don't try sticking your finger in a flytrap. It won't hurt *you*. But you could hurt or kill the plant.

Venus flytraps grow in bogs and damp, mossy areas in North and South Carolina. The dirt in these bogs doesn't have enough nitrogen to keep the plant healthy. So the flytrap developed its taste for insects and spiders. They give the plant the nitrogen it needs. The Venus flytrap also gets protein from these meals.

The Venus flytrap catches its supper with special pairs of hinged leaves. They look like sets of jaws, or very small bear traps. The edges of the leaves have long spikes. There are tiny hairs on the leaves of each trap. When a curious insect wanders along a leaf, it brushes against these hairs. The contact triggers the trap. The leaves clamp together. They snap shut faster than you can snap your fingers. Chomp!

It takes the plant about ten days to digest its unlucky prey. The flytrap makes chemicals that dissolve the trapped bug or spider. The plant absorbs nutrients from the prey's body.

The Venus flytrap gets its name from Venus, the Roman goddess of love. This might sound strange. After all, this toothy plant doesn't seem very loving. On the other hand, you *could* say that it really loves bugs.

From *Building Character with True Stories from Nature* by Barbara A. Lewis, copyright © 2012. Free Spirit Publishing Inc., Minneapolis, MN; 800-735-7323; www.freespirit.com. This page may be reproduced for use within an individual classroom. For all other uses, contact www.freespirit.com/company/permissions.cfm.

Talk It Over

Use these questions to guide your students in considering analogies between Venus flytraps and self-control, good decision-making, and other character traits and behaviors in people.

The Venus flytrap adapted to living in boggy areas by eating insects. Can you make an analogy to the ways people show adaptability?

- It can be hard to adapt to a new place or a new situation. Sometimes we need to come up with creative ways to deal with change. Creativity and imagination are part of adaptability.

- People who have challenges in some areas of their lives can adapt to their situations and overcome these challenges. They can learn other skills to help them succeed. (For examples of this kind of adaptability, see pages 43, 54, and 112.)

- Sometimes we can help others adapt to new situations. For example, kids can help new students adjust by showing them around school, sitting with them at lunch, and being friendly to them.

Curious bugs that crawl along the Venus flytrap's hinged, spiny leaves may become lunch for the plant. Can you make an analogy to the way people act when they are curious? How can self-control help protect us from situations that could become dangerous?

- You might be curious about a new or unfamiliar place or activity. Curiosity is natural and can lead to exciting discoveries. But if you're not careful and don't make safe decisions, or if you don't exercise self-control, you might put yourself or someone else at risk. It's important to think carefully about your choices and consider the consequences.

- If you get too close to dangerous activities, you might be trapped and find it hard to escape. For example, if you try using drugs, or if you spend time with people who get into fights, you could get caught up in a scary situation. You may have a hard time getting away. But if you turn to trusted adults for help, you can find the strength and help you need to break free.

The Venus flytrap gets its name from the ancient Roman goddess of love. But in many ways, this plant doesn't seem exactly "loving." Do people ever make assumptions about others based on their names or appearances? Do you think this is a good idea?

- Sometimes when we hear a person's name or learn about just one part of his or her life, we make assumptions about what the person is like. But everyone has many different sides. One aspect of someone's personality is not the whole story.

- A person who seems very different from you at first might turn out to be a great friend. You can never be sure what someone is like until you get to know him or her.

- Names and appearances can be deceptive. It's best not to make assumptions about people. What sounds good might be harmful, and what looks attractive might be danger in disguise.

The Venus flytrap can snag insects before they know what has hit them. Can you compare this quick turn of events to the way people make decisions?

- Sometimes you might make a snap decision and then regret it. It's important to take responsibility for your choice, and use the experience to make a better decision next time.

- You shouldn't flirt with danger. If you get too close to danger, you might get hurt. Make good decisions to keep yourself and others safe. And if you're not sure what to do, talk to a trusted adult.

- It's a good idea to think about possible consequences of an action before making a decision. Still, we can't always know or control what will happen, and we all make poor choices sometimes. It's part of being human.

Venus Flytrap Facts

The leaves of the Venus flytrap produce a sweet nectar that attracts insects to the plant.

In addition to capturing spiders and insects, Venus flytraps sometimes catch and digest small frogs.

If a trap catches a falling leaf or something else that is not food for the plant, the trap will reopen in twelve to twenty-four hours.

Activities

Activity 1: Character Dilemmas

Materials

None

Directions

Explain to kids that a dilemma is a situation in which you could make more than one choice. These choices might be good, bad, or a mixture of both. The most difficult choices occur when two positive character traits come into conflict with each other. Can you always be both honest and loyal, for example?

Discuss a few character dilemmas with your class. Ask how kids would react in each situation, and why. Explain that all choices have consequences, and that people need to take responsibility for their own choices. How can we know what the right decision is? *Is* there always a "right" decision? A few sample dilemmas follow. Feel free to add any others that you'd like.

- Your best friend cheats on a test. Should you stay loyal to your friend and not tell anyone, or should you be honest and tell the teacher? What are the possible consequences of each decision?

- You are home with your brother, and no grown-ups are home. You're writing a report about magnets. It's due tomorrow, and you've waited until the last minute to work on it. You don't have any books about magnets in the house, and it's too late to go to the library. You think you could find information online, though. You've always been taught to be responsible and get your homework done. But your mom has also told you never to use the Internet unless an adult is home. You trust yourself to stay away from unsafe websites, but you'd still be breaking your mom's rule about not using the Internet without a grown-up. What should you do? How can you be responsible about your homework and also obey your mom? If you can't do both, which do you think is more important?

- You're at a birthday party, and some of your friends are going to sneak away and watch a scary movie that they took from someone's older sister. They want you to come along. A little voice in your head tells you not to go. You have a bad feeling about it, but you don't know why. You really want to go with your friends, because you like them and you want them to like you. Plus, you're curious about what the movie will be like. Do you listen to that little voice, or do you go with your friends? What character traits are involved in making this decision?

Variation: Hold a panel discussion about dilemmas. Ask three or four students to sit at the front of the room. Pose sample dilemmas to them and ask what each of them would do. Then invite kids in the audience to ask questions and share their own thoughts.

Activity 2: Flytrap Words

Materials

Slips of paper

Hat, bowl, or other container

Preparation

Play a game in which students have to give each other clues to guess certain words, without saying these target "Flytrap Words" themselves. For example, if Michaela is trying to get Cameron to guess the word *flower*, Michaela could give hints such as *blossom* or *rose*. Or Michaela could go a different route and say *ingredient in bread*, to get Cameron to say the homonym, *flour*.

Before playing, write Flytrap Words on slips of paper. Choose enough words so that you have four for every two students. So, if you have a class of twenty-four, you would need forty-eight words. These don't have to be especially complicated or clever. Sometimes the simplest words and concepts can be the hardest to guess. If you like, some of your Flytrap Words could be related to the lesson. You could also mix in vocabulary or spelling words that your class is working on. For example, Flytrap Words might include *fly, happy, train, spider, stop sign, plant, writer, leaves, yellow, frog, ancient, magnet, teeth, neighborhood,* and *orange juice.* Fold the slips in half and place them all in a hat or other container.

Directions

Pair kids up and explain the idea behind the game. Tell them that each round will last two minutes, and kids will take turns being prompters and guessers. If the timer runs out for a round before the Flytrap Word is guessed, or if the prompting student says the Flytrap Word then, snap! The flytrap closes, and the team gets no points for that round. At the end of four rounds, whichever team has the most points is the winner.

Then walk around the room and ask one student from each pair to draw a slip and wait to look at it until you say it's time. When every team has a slip, start the timer for two minutes and tell the students

with the slips that they can now look at their words and start giving clues.

You'll soon notice that the kids doing the prompting will have to control the urge to blurt out the answers, which can be especially difficult if it's taking other players a long time to guess correctly. In addition, with each round, kids will need to stay adaptable and flexible as they switch back and forth between being prompters and guessers.

After the game, ask kids if they found the game challenging. As prompter, how hard was it not to say the Flytrap Words? How hard was it to be the guesser? Which role did kids prefer, and why? Discuss the fact that it's not always easy to show self-control, especially if we feel stressed or pressured in a situation. Talk about ways kids can practice and improve self-control in their lives, such as writing lists of tasks and priorities to help them decide whether they have time to watch a movie; setting a schedule for exercise, homework, or chores; or testing themselves by trying to go without something that tempts them (whether it's ice cream or video games) for a certain amount of time.

Activity 3: Feed a Flytrap

Materials

Venus flytrap

Pot

Peat moss

Sand

Preparation

Buy a Venus flytrap from a local nursery or online at sites such as www.petflytrap.com, www.flytrapstore.com, or www.californiacarnivores.com. *Note:* If you repot a Venus flytrap, do not use regular gardening soil, which can kill the plant. Venus flytraps grow best in a mixture of peat moss and sand, with no fertilizer. Also, water your flytrap with distilled water, rainwater, or reverse osmosis water, and be sure the pot allows the water to drain.

Place the potted flytrap in your classroom.

Directions

Show students the toothy new addition to your classroom. Talk about how the Venus flytrap catches and digests its prey. Have kids take turns watering the plant. If desired, kids can also take turns catching insects and feeding them to the plant, or you can do this yourself. (*Note:* Warn kids never to put their fingers, or anything other than a small insect, into any of the plant's traps. They can hurt or even kill the plant or its traps this way.)

Watching the Venus flytrap in action will help bring some of this lesson's analogies to life.

Periodically, once kids have had a few chances to observe the flytrap catching and digesting prey, talk with kids about analogies to human behavior and character. For example, after kids have seen the plant catch an insect, you could talk about the way it can be easy to get too close to danger when we're curious about something, someplace, or someone. You could then extend this analogy to explore the need to make good decisions and to be accountable for the consequences of our actions. You can also use the example of kids taking turns caring for the plant to discuss responsibility.

Lesson 25
Wolves

Character Key Words
Loyalty • Trustworthiness • Caring • Cooperation • Service

Students will
- learn about wolves and some of their characteristics, such as the way pack members care for each other, and make analogies to traits such as trustworthiness and loyalty among people
- draw analogies between wolf behavior and people who serve others in need
- consider what can happen when people are kind and helpful to others and also discuss when it's better to get help from an adult
- understand the way wolves cooperate within the pack to support and care for all members, and make analogies to people who cooperate in families, schools, and communities

Overview
Wolves are often viewed as dangerous animals, and many frightening stories describe attacks on people. The wolf's eerie howl has probably helped inspire such stories. But in reality—while wolves do hunt and eat many animals, from elk and deer to foxes and fish—they are very rarely aggressive toward humans.

Kids will be fascinated by the highly social and structured nature of wolf packs and the way pack members cooperate and care for each other. They'll also be intrigued by wolves' loyalty to their packs and to their mates. Exploring these behaviors with your group is a great way to spark meaningful discussion about positive character traits such as citizenship and trust.

Story
Wild Wolves

Wild Wolves

Have you ever heard of a *lone wolf*? It usually describes someone who likes to work and play alone. But where does this phrase come from?

The idea of a lone wolf comes from the way wolves live in the wild. Most of the time, wolves are not alone. They live in family groups called packs. About five to eleven wolves live in the same pack. The main male and female in the pack are mates. Wolf mates are very loyal to each other. They usually stay together for life. This pair leads the pack.

Sometimes, the pack drives out a young male wolf. Then he becomes a lone wolf. Other times, male wolves leave to start their own packs. Wolves need packs, because they hunt animals that are much bigger than they are, such as moose and elk. Wolves work together to hunt and bring down these large prey.

Wolves also work together in other ways. Adult wolves help take care of the pack's babies, called pups. Wolf pups are very playful. Playing helps them learn how to be adult wolves. They learn how to hunt and how to communicate through sounds, posture, and facial expressions. They learn to be good members of the pack.

Wolves are close relatives of dogs. Thousands of years ago, humans began taming some wild gray wolves. Slowly, these tame wolves evolved into the dogs we know today. Sometimes wolves will mate with dogs. Their babies are half wolf and half dog.

Eve and Norman Fertig met one of these wolf dogs. The Fertigs are animal lovers. They rescue and care for animals that are hurt or sick. One day they came across a two-week-old wolf dog. She was very sick. The Fertigs named her Shana and kept her as a pet. They saved Shana's life. They didn't know that Shana would return the favor one day.

From *Building Character with True Stories from Nature* by Barbara A. Lewis, copyright © 2012. Free Spirit Publishing Inc., Minneapolis, MN; 800-735-7323; www.freespirit.com. This page may be reproduced for use within an individual classroom. For all other uses, contact www.freespirit.com/company/permissions.cfm.

A few years later a huge winter storm hit their area. When the storm came, the Fertigs were outside on their land. Trees fell everywhere. Snow blanketed the ground. The Fertigs couldn't get back to their house. They were freezing cold. They were afraid they would die.

But then Shana saved the day. She dug a tunnel underneath the snow and fallen trees, all the way to their house. Then the 160-pound wolf dog carried Eve on her back through the tunnel and pulled Norman along behind her. The Fertigs say Shana saved their lives.

Lots of people live with dogs. Some, like the Fertigs, even have wolf dogs in their homes. But have you ever known someone who went out and lived with wolves? A man named Shaun Ellis did this. First he studied wolves. Then he wanted to get closer. Shaun took a big risk. He moved into the wild and began living near a wolf pack. In time, the wolves learned that Shaun wouldn't hurt them. They grew to trust him. They even brought him food to eat. In return, Shaun babysat the pack's wolf pups.

One day, Shaun wanted to get a drink from a nearby stream. But one of the wolves stopped him right in his tracks. The wolf snarled. He nipped at Shaun. Shaun was scared. Had the wolves turned against him? But the wolf didn't hurt Shaun.

Later, Shaun did go to the stream. Guess what he saw? Bear tracks. Shaun realized that the wolf had probably saved his life. The wolf had also protected the lives of the pack's pups. The bear might have followed Shaun's tracks or his scent back to the den where the pups played.

Shaun and the wolves trusted and protected each other, like members of the same pack. They were a team. Who belongs to *your* pack?

From *Building Character with True Stories from Nature* by Barbara A. Lewis, copyright © 2012. Free Spirit Publishing Inc., Minneapolis, MN; 800-735-7323; www.freespirit.com.
This page may be reproduced for use within an individual classroom. For all other uses, contact www.freespirit.com/company/permissions.cfm.

Talk It Over

Use these questions to guide your students in considering analogies between wolves and caring, loyalty, and other character traits and behaviors in people.

Sometimes a wolf leaves his pack or is driven away. Then he becomes a lone wolf. Lone wolves may be more aggressive than wolves in packs, because they have to fight harder for their food. Can you compare and contrast these ideas to situations people might be in?

- Everyone needs to be alone sometimes. Just because a person wants some privacy or some quiet time doesn't mean that he or she is unfriendly.

- Being alone and being lonely are different. When we're lonely, we may also feel very sad. If you feel sad and lonely a lot, talk to a grown-up you trust.

- If people are unkind to someone and don't let him or her play with them or join their group, that person might feel hurt and angry. If you're ever tempted to exclude someone else, think about how you would feel in his or her place. It's important to be kind to others.

Wolves are very loyal to the members of their packs and especially to their mates. Can you compare this to human examples of loyalty?

- Family members are usually loyal to each other.

- True friends are loyal to each other. They stick up for each other and they are honest with each other.

- People often feel loyalty to groups they belong to, such as schools, clubs, faith communities, and nations. Loyalty can help these groups be stronger and more successful. But lasting loyalty must be earned. If people feel betrayed by someone or something they've been loyal to, they may be very angry or sad.

Wolves in the same pack help care for young pups. And wolves work together to hunt moose and other large animals. If pack members don't work together for the good of the group, they all suffer. **Can you compare this to behaviors or situations among people?**

- Every member of a family has responsibilities and chores, from parents to young kids. Without cooperation, the family wouldn't function as well.

- Schools, communities, and governments need to all work together to make sure all citizens are cared for.

- Some jobs are a lot easier to do with help. Having other people around can make a job more fun, too.

Every member of a wolf pack has to count on the other members for support. Living together and relying on each other this way takes trust. How can people build trust in each other?

- When you are honest, people are more likely to trust you.

- People will trust you more if you are dependable and do what you say you will do. If you promise to clean your room or help a friend with a project and then go back on your word, you might lose other people's trust.

- Being kind and caring can earn the trust of others over time.

- In a family, class, or community, everyone's success is connected. Cooperation and good citizenship are positive traits that can help everyone succeed.

Shaun lived safely with wolves. And Shana, a wolf dog, saved Eve and Norman's lives. But many people think of wolves as dangerous and wouldn't have rescued a wolf dog like Shana. What can happen when we show kindness to someone? When might it be better to play it safe or get help?

- If you are kind and caring toward a person you don't know well, he or she might become your friend.

- If you help someone out, he or she might feel very loyal to you. That person might also be there for you someday when *you* need help.

- If you see someone being bullied, you can stand up for that person and be his or her friend. But if you feel afraid, don't confront the person doing the bullying. Get help from a grown-up.

- It is important to help people who need it. But sometimes the best way to help is by going to a grown-up. For example, if you see a person who seems to be drowning, you should never get into the water. It's not safe. Instead, you should call for help.

- Wild animals are not pets. Shaun's story is unusual. So is the story of Shana. You should never be cruel to an animal. But it's also important to be very careful around wild animals, or around any animals that you aren't familiar with.

Wolf Facts

There are three main kinds of wolves: the gray wolf, the red wolf, and the maned wolf. The gray wolf is the most common.

Some experts think that wolves mourn when a pack member dies. The pack may howl as though they're calling for the dead wolf. The wolf's mate, especially, may seem to grieve for a long time.

When a wolf pack catches a large animal, an adult wolf may eat up to 20 pounds of meat in a single meal. That would be like eating eighty hamburgers or more in one sitting!

Activities

Activity 1: Wolf Book Club

Materials

Chosen book (1 copy per student, or 1 to read aloud as a group)

Directions

Choose a book about wolves that is suited to your students' ages and abilities. Options include *Wolf Island* (for grades 1 through 4) by Celia Godkin, *Look to the North: A Wolf Pup Diary* (for kindergarten through grade 3) or *Julie of the Wolves* (for grades 4 and up) by Jean Craighead George, *Summer of the Wolves* (for grades 5 and up) by Polly Carlson-Voiles, or *White Fang* (for grades 5 and up) by Jack London.

Kids can read the chosen book individually, or you can read it aloud as a group. In either case, hold regular "wolf book club" meetings during the course of reading the book. Gather kids in a circle and talk about the story as a group. Consider the way wolves are portrayed. Focus on examples of wolf loyalty, trust, cooperation, and service to others or to the pack. Also talk about the way the people are shown (if at all). What were kids' favorite—and least favorite—parts of the story, and why? Why do they think the writer made the decisions that he or she did? What are some other ways the story might have gone?

If desired, end this activity by having kids write their own stories about wolves.

Activity 2: Good Question!

Materials

Good Question! handout (on CD-ROM)

Directions

Pass out copies of the Good Question! handout and tell kids that they'll each be interviewing a family member or other adult. Ask them to focus their interviews on topics such as family, loyalty, and trust. As a group, brainstorm interview questions. For example, *Growing up, what family member did you feel closest to, and why?* or *When was a time you really had to trust someone?*

Once you have a list of ten questions or so, have each student write down on the handout three to five questions that he or she finds most interesting. Tell kids that they can use these questions as starting points in their interviews, but also encourage them to tailor their questions according to the people they interview and where their conversations go. Explain that interviewers need to listen closely to answers and think about what their next questions should be. Remind kids that wolves communicate through sounds, and also through facial expressions and body language. People do this, too. So, as they conduct their interviews, kids can watch for what their interviewees are saying *without* words.

After kids have done their interviews, talk about the activity. Was it harder than kids expected to conduct an interesting and productive interview? Did they learn things that surprised them? Did they enjoy the experience of being interviewers?

Variation: Ask kids to write essays, articles, or stories based on what they learned in their interviews. If kids feel comfortable doing so, they can share these with the class.

Activity 3: Adopt a Wolf

Materials
Various

Directions
Wolves in the wild need help. Explain to kids that wolves are endangered or threatened in many parts of the world. And we—humans—are their most dangerous predators. Humans have hunted and trapped wolves for many years. In addition, construction and other human activities have disrupted wolves' habitat.

Fortunately, kids can make a difference! As a group, brainstorm ways to raise money to "adopt" a wolf (through the World Wildlife Fund, for example) or to donate to a sanctuary or other organization that helps protect and care for wolves, such as the International Wolf Center (www.wolf.org). Fundraising ideas might include raking yards, holding a bake sale, selling raffle tickets to win wolf prizes (a book about wolves, a toy wolf, etc.), or putting on a play about wolves and charging admission.

Once you have a list of ideas, choose a few that look possible for your group, and ask kids to vote on their favorite. Then develop an action plan for carrying out this service project. Talk about what supplies you'll need, how much time it will take to organize and hold the event, and who could help.

After you hold your event, talk with kids about the experience. Did they succeed in reaching their goal? Are there things they would do differently next time? How did it feel to help wolves? Did this service project give them ideas for additional ways to help wolves or other animals?

Character Key Word Glossary

adaptability: the ability to change to make different situations easier

assertiveness: speaking up in a strong but polite way

balance: when the different parts of a person's life are in harmony with each other; for example, if you have balance in your life, you have time for school and homework, having fun with friends, after-school activities, and family

caring: showing that you care about someone; showing concern, being kind, sharing, helping, and giving are all ways that you show you care

citizenship: being a member of a community, state, province, or country; the way you act as a member of a community

communication: sharing information, thoughts, or feelings with someone else by saying it out loud, writing it, or showing an example

conservation: protecting or saving something, especially related to our planet and environment; for example, recycling paper to keep more trees from being cut down to make new paper

cooperation: working and playing together peacefully; working together on a job or on a problem that needs to be solved

courage: braveness; boldness; doing something that is positive, even if it feels scary

curiosity: having questions about something new or something you don't understand; being interested in learning more

fairness and equality: treating other people the way you would like to be treated; giving everyone the kinds of rights and chances you have; when you're fair, you do your best to share, take turns, and treat each person with respect.

forgiveness: the act of forgiving someone; giving up hurt or anger toward someone

friendship: the connection or tie you have with someone you care about and like to do things with

good decision-making: using good judgment and making positive choices; knowing when something doesn't feel right

hard work: dedication and commitment to a task; being willing to do a difficult job

helpfulness: willingness to help; offering help even when it's not asked for

honesty: truthfulness

inner strength: being true to yourself; standing up for your beliefs no matter what

integrity: being yourself; being honest with yourself and others; doing what you say you will do; having strong values and sticking to them

loyalty: being devoted and faithful; standing by someone

patience: being calm; the ability to wait for someone or for something to happen; the ability to see something through to the end

peacefulness: inner calmness; knowing how to work through disagreements; working together to solve problems

perseverance: practicing until it's right; trying over and over again; never giving up

planning and preparation: figuring out ahead of time how to do something so it goes well; getting ready for a task ahead of time

playfulness: having fun; a positive, happy attitude; a good sense of humor

problem solving: trying different solutions until you find something that works; making choices and accepting the consequences even when your choices don't turn out the way you want them to

respect: care and concern for others and yourself; when you respect someone, you care about the person's ideas, thoughts, and feelings

responsibility: the act of making good choices, being dependable, and taking charge of your own actions, words, and thoughts

safety: being free from harm or risk

self-control: being able to make decisions without direction from others; doing the right thing on your own, without a teacher or parent telling you to; resisting temptation

service: a kind act that you do for people, animals, or the environment

tolerance and acceptance: caring about people no matter who they are or what their beliefs are; including people even if they are different; liking people for who they are without trying to change them

trust: believing that someone is there for you; depending on someone; counting on someone to do what he or she says he or she will do

trustworthiness: people are able to count on you to do what you say you'll do; dependability

wisdom and learning: appreciation for the value of learning, all throughout life; using your knowledge and experience to grow and be a better person

References and Resources

Books for Kids

These resources, both fiction and nonfiction, explore the animals and plants in *Building Character with True Stories from Nature*. While not all of these books discuss character education directly, you can use the ideas within them to explore character with your students and spark meaningful discussion about positive traits and behavior, as well as to further investigate these fascinating animals and plants.

Apes

Apes Escape! And More True Stories of Animals Behaving Badly by Aline Alexander Newman (Washington, DC: National Geographic Children's Books, 2012). Fu Manchu is an orangutan that outwits zookeepers and picks locks so he can break out of his habitat and wander the Omaha Zoo. Fu Manchu even makes his own lock-picking tool, which he hides in his mouth so he won't be caught. This book also contains two other stories about resourceful animals. *Grades 2 and up; nonfiction.*

Koko's Kitten by Dr. Francine Patterson (New York: Scholastic, 1985). When Koko, a great ape fluent in sign language, asks her trainer for a kitten, the trainer buys a toy kitten. But Koko wants a real, live kitten, and when her wish is finally granted, she grooms and cuddles the kitten she names All Ball. When All Ball is run over by a car, Koko grieves in a way that humans can relate to. *Grades K–3; nonfiction.*

Bamboo

Life Cycles: Bamboo by Julie K. Lundgren (Vero Beach, FL: Rourke Publishing, 2011). Students will be guided through the complete life cycle of bamboo. *Grades 2 and up; nonfiction.*

Box Jellyfish

The Box Jellyfish by Colleen Sexton (Minneapolis: Bellwether Media, 2011). The box jellyfish, also called the sea wasp, is full of toxin. Each of its tentacles has 5,000 sting cells with enough poison to kill sixty people! In this book, young readers will discover what makes the box jellyfish one of the ocean's most beautiful but terrifying creatures. *Grades 3 and up; nonfiction.*

Bristlecone Pine Trees

Bristlecone Pines by Kelli M. Brucken (Farmington Hills, MI: KidHaven Press, 2005). Bristlecone pines manage not only to survive through the hottest heat and coldest cold, they thrive and are the world's oldest living trees. Kids will learn how these trees grow and why they must be protected. *Grades 4 and up; nonfiction.*

Cats

The Cats of Roxville Station by Jean Craighead George (New York: Dutton Juvenile, 2009). Rachet the cat is thrown into a river, but she doesn't drown—she is able to climb her way up the riverbank and find a new home with a group of feral cats by the Roxville train station. Soon Rachet meets a foster child named Mike, who wants to be her friend—but first he must gain her trust. *Grades 4–6; fiction.*

Dewey the Library Cat by Vicki Myron and Bret Witter (New York: Little, Brown, 2010). Dewey the cat was left in a library book drop slot on the coldest night of the year and managed to survive. Named Dewey Readmore Books by his new caregivers, he gained many new friends and fans and inspired library-goers with his winning spirit. *Grades 4–8; nonfiction.*

The Famous Nini: A Mostly True Story of How a Plain White Cat Became a Star by Mary Nethery (New York: Clarion Books, 2010). Nini is a stray cat until she is taken in by a café owner in Venice. Soon Nini becomes famous and charms equally famous fans such as Giuseppe Verdi and the pope. But it is the little girl she comforts who will touch the hearts of young readers. *Grades K–2; fiction.*

Coconut Crabs

Crabs by Mary Jo Rhodes and David Hall (New York: Scholastic, 2007). Chockful of dramatic photos and fascinating facts about crabs, this book will teach kids about coconut crabs and many other crabs. *Grades 2 and up; nonfiction.*

Crows

Crows! Strange and Wonderful by Laurence Pringle (Honesdale, PA: Boyds Mill Press, 2010). Crows have a remarkable way of communicating with one another, using at least twenty-five distinct sounds to get their messages across. Children will learn how crows "talk," behave, and survive. *Grades 2 and up; nonfiction.*

The Summer of the Crows: Not Your Typical Boy Meets Crow Story by Tony Ducklow (Amazon Digital Services, 2011). When Tucker McNeal happens upon baby crows orphaned by a summer storm, the experience turns into an adventure that teaches him about the amazing intelligence of crows. *Grades 4 and up; fiction.*

Dandelions

A Dandelion's Life by John Himmelman (New York: Children's Press, 1998). This picture book takes readers through the dandelion's life cycle, from seed to blossom and back to seed. *Grades K and up; nonfiction.*

The Dandelion Seed by Joseph Anthony (Nevada City, CA: Dawn Publications, 1997). This picture book takes kids on a journey with a dandelion seed that is afraid to leave its flower when autumn comes. *Grades K and up; fiction.*

Dogs

Along Came a Dog by Meindert DeJong (New York: HarperCollins, 1980). In this book illustrated by Maurice Sendak, a homeless dog takes it upon himself to protect a little red hen, and the two become friends. *Grades 3 and up; fiction.*

Because of Winn-Dixie by Kate DiCamillo (Cambridge, MA: Candlewick Press, 2000). Winn-Dixie is a big, ugly dog that teaches ten-year-old Opal about her absent mother, helps her make new friends in her new hometown, and makes her feel happier and less alone. *Grades 4 and up; fiction.*

The Call of the Wild by Jack London (New York: Macmillan Company, 1903). In this classic novel set during the Alaska Gold Rush, a heroic dog must decide whether to answer the call of the wild or to live with humans. *Grades 4 and up; fiction.*

Hachiko Waits by Lesléa Newman (New York: Henry Holt, 2004). Based on the true story of loyal Hachiko, the Akita dog that waited for his owner at a train station in Japan, long after his owner had died. *Grades 3–5; fiction.*

More than Man's Best Friend: The Story of Working Dogs by Robyn O'Sullivan (Washington, DC: National Geographic Children's Books, 2006). Dogs aren't just playful pets—some also work hard as guide dogs, service dogs, customs dogs, herders, and search-and-rescue dogs. *Grades 1 and up; nonfiction.*

Nubs: The True Story of a Mutt, a Marine & a Miracle by Brian Dennis, Mary Nethery, and Kirby Larson (New York: Little, Brown, 2009). Nubs was the leader of a pack of wild dogs in Iraq when he was befriended by Marine Major Brian Dennis. When Major Dennis and the Marines were relocated 70 miles away, Nubs showed up. Because the Marines aren't allowed to have pets, Major Dennis arranged for Nubs to stay with a family in the United States until Dennis could return home and take Nubs in as his own. *Grades 3–5; nonfiction.*

Shelter Dogs: Amazing Stories of Adopted Strays by Peg Kehret (Morton Grove, IL: Albert Whitman & Company, 1999). This book shares the individual stories of eight stray dogs that were left at animal shelters, were adopted by loving families, and went on to thrive and prove how amazing dogs can be. *Grades 3–6; nonfiction.*

Shiloh by Phyllis Reynolds Naylor (New York: Antheneum, 1991). Marty Preston finds a beagle in the hills behind his home and promptly names him Shiloh. But he soon learns that Shiloh belongs to someone else, a man who drinks too much, has a gun, and abuses his dogs. Marty finds himself in a dangerous ethical dilemma when Shiloh's angry owner wants him back. *Grades 3 and up; fiction.*

Where the Red Fern Grows: The Story of Two Dogs and a Boy by Wilson Rawls (Garden City, NY: Doubleday, 1961). Billy Colman and his hound dogs roam the Ozarks, hunting for a raccoon Billy hopes to enter in an annual raccoon hunt contest, fighting a mountain lion in the process, a clash that ends tragically. Billy finds peace in the Native American legend of the sacred red fern that grows over the graves of his dogs. *Grades 4 and up; fiction.*

Dolphins

Dolphin Adventure: A True Story by Wayne Grover (New York: Greenwillow Books, 2000). The author shares his encounter with a dolphin family of three, a mother, father, and baby, off the Atlantic coast of Florida. Upon discovering that the baby dolphin is trapped because its tail has been wound in fishing line and its flesh pierced with a hook, Grover dives underwater to free it with his diving knife. The blood from the dolphin's injury attracts two sharks that the father dolphin attacks, saving Grover's life. *Grades 3 and up; nonfiction.*

Island of the Blue Dolphins by Scott O'Dell (Boston: Houghton Mifflin, 1960). Karana lives alone on an island, where she not only survives sometimes harsh conditions but thrives in serene solitude. *Grades 4 and up; fiction.*

The Music of Dolphins by Karen Hesse (New York: Scholastic Press, 1996). Mila lives with dolphins on a deserted island until the Coast Guard finds her. She is soon subjected to a government study, during which she is taught about language and music. Mila's progress in the "real world" is impressive, but she feels drawn to her island home. *Grades 4–8; fiction.*

Nine True Dolphin Stories by Margaret Davidson (New York: Scholastic Educational, 2004). Included in this collection of true stories about dolphins—one that gives children rides on her back, and another that is trained to save lives—are facts about how dolphins survive and how scientists study them. *Grades 3–5; nonfiction.*

One White Dolphin by Gill Lewis (New York: Atheneum, 2012). Kara and her family are dedicated to protecting marine life and saving the reef, which causes problems with Jake and his family, because fishermen need to dredge the reef in order to make a living. Kara soon meets a boy named Felix, who hopes to sail in the Paralympics. Felix and Kara work together to save a baby albino dolphin caught in a fishing net, an act that has interesting results for the reef. *Grades 3 and up; fiction.*

Winter's Tail: How One Little Dolphin Learned to Swim Again by Craig Hatkoff, Isabella Hatkoff, and Juliana Hatkoff (New York: Scholastic Press, 2009). Winter the dolphin was caught in a crab trap when she was a baby, seriously injuring her tail. She was rescued, but her tail eventually fell off. With the help of a prosthetic tail, Winter was able to swim again, and has been an inspiration to young amputees. *Dolphin Tale*, starring Harry Connick Jr., Ashley Judd, and Morgan Freeman, came out in 2011. *Grades 3–5; nonfiction.*

Dragonflies

Are You a Dragonfly? by Judy Allen and Tudor Humphries (Boston: Kingfisher Publications, 2001). This picture book explores the life cycle, habits, and features of dragonflies. *Grades K and up; nonfiction.*

Take a Walk with Butterflies and Dragonflies by Jane Kirkland (Lionville, PA: Stillwater Publishing, 2004). Young readers will learn about the stages of life butterflies and dragonflies go through—eggs, larvae, and adults—the differences between dragonflies and damselflies and butterflies and moths, and how they survive. *Grades 4 and up; nonfiction.*

Elephants

An Elephant in the Garden by Michael Morpurgo (New York: Feiwell and Friends, 2011). In this wartime novel, a zoo-keeping family decides to save an elephant named Marlene rather than allow her to be destroyed with the other animals so they don't run wild if the zoo is bombed. Marlene will stay in the family's garden instead, until the city is bombed and they must flee—with an elephant. *Grades 5 and up; fiction.*

Elephant Talk: The Surprising Science of Elephant Communication by Ann Downer (Minneapolis: Twenty First Century Books, 2011). Elephants may not talk the way humans do, but scientists have found that they have a unique way of communicating with one another, even when separated. The author examines this communication and its possible impact on the dwindling population of elephants due to poaching. *Grades 3 and up; nonfiction.*

Tarra & Bella: The Elephant and Dog Who Became Best Friends by Carol Buckley (New York: G.P. Putnam's Sons, 2009). Tarra the elephant has retired from the circus and moved to the Elephant Sanctuary of Tennessee, where she is a loner until she meets a stray dog named Bella. The other elephants have paired up with each other, but Tarra and Bella bond as an unlikely but inseparable duo. *Grades 3–6; nonfiction.*

Fireflies

Fireflies! by Julie Brinckloe (New York: Aladdin Books, 1986). A young boy catches enough fireflies to fill a jar, and he is fascinated by the light they cast. He soon realizes, however, that if he doesn't release them from the jar they will die. *Grades K and up; fiction.*

Fireflies by Megan E. Bryant (New York: Grosset & Dunlap, 2008). Kids will learn interesting facts about fireflies and how to make their yard a welcome place for them. *Grades 1 and up; nonfiction.*

Horses

Black Beauty by Anna Sewell (New York: Hurst and Company, 1903). A classic with the unique twist of a horse for a narrator, this book follows the life of Black Beauty, from colt to carriage horse to cab horse. Readers will see how some people treat animals very well and others abuse them, and how the animal might be affected. *Grades 4 and up; fiction.*

Goliath: Hero of the Great Baltimore Fire by Claudia Friddell (Ann Arbor, MI: Sleeping Bear Press, 2010). The Great Baltimore Fire of 1904 is often overshadowed by the Great Chicago Fire, but it caused considerable destruction. Goliath, the huge horse from Engine Company 15, endured an explosion and then pulled a fire rig to safety—by himself. *Grades K–5; nonfiction.*

War Horse by Michael Morpurgo (New York: Greenwillow Books, 1982). Now a well-known and well-awarded movie directed by Steven Spielberg, the novel follows Joey, a bay-red foal, through his journey across Europe as part of the army. He has left behind his beloved owner, a boy named Albert, and their painful separation is detailed with warmth. *Grades 5 and up; fiction.*

Moths

Eyewitness: Butterfly & Moth by DK Publishing (New York: DK Children, 2000). Using photographs to document the life cycle of moths and butterflies, this book will teach young readers about where these insects live, what they eat, and how they survive. *Grades 3 and up; nonfiction.*

Parrots

Alex the Parrot: No Ordinary Bird by Stephanie Spinner (New York: Alfred A. Knopf, 2012). In 1977, most scientists figured parrots' small brains equaled limited intelligence. But Irene Pepperberg, a graduate student interested in studying the African gray parrot, bought one of her own and named him Alex, short for Avian Learning EXperiment. Pepperberg soon realized that Alex had a great capacity to learn. *Grades 3 and up; nonfiction.*

Penguins

March of the Penguins by Luc Jacquet (Washington, DC: National Geographic Children's Books, 2006). The book version of the impressive documentary follows emperor penguins as they journey across the Antarctic to hatch and raise their chicks. *Grades 3 and up; nonfiction.*

My Season with Penguins: An Antarctic Journal by Sophie Webb (New York: Sandpiper, 2004). The author shares her experience of living in the Antarctic with Adélie penguins for two months, including being slapped by one of the hardy birds. *Grades 4–8; nonfiction.*

The World of Penguins by Evelyne Daigle (Plattsburgh, NY: Tundra Books, 2008). Readers will learn about all kinds of penguins living in and through all kinds of situations, aided by realistic acrylic paintings and photos. They will read about where penguins nest and what they eat, as well as who wants to eat them. *Grades 4 and up; nonfiction.*

Pigs

Ace: The Very Important Pig by Dick King-Smith (New York: Crown Publishers, 1992). Ace isn't like the other piglets in his litter: not only does he have a black mark like a club from a deck of cards, he can understand Farmer Tubbs when he talks to him. When Ace wants something, he grunts, making different sounds depending on what he is trying to communicate. Soon Ace has made himself comfortable in the farmer's house, where he watches TV and spends time with his friends, a house cat and a dog. *Grades 3–5; fiction.*

Babe: The Gallant Pig by Dick King-Smith (New York: Crown, 1985). Babe the pig is taken in by Farmer Hogget's sheepdog, Fly, and he learns how to herd sheep himself. When Babe manages to save the sheep from rustlers and wild dogs, Farmer Hoggett is convinced that the pig is a worthy sheep "dog." The sweet, sincere pig is soon entered into the Grand Challenge Sheepdog Trials. *Grades 4 and up; fiction.*

Charlotte's Web by E.B. White (New York: Harper, 1952). Kids will love getting to know Wilbur and Charlotte, and if they've already read this classic tale at home they'll be happy to get reacquainted. In an attempt to save Wilbur the pig from becoming bacon, Charlotte the spider begins spinning webs with persuasive messages woven in. The side characters—the other farm animals—add to the charming story. *Grades 3–5; fiction.*

Quaking Aspens

Quaking Aspen by Bonnie Holmes (Minneapolis: Carolrhoda Books, 1999). Kids will learn about the quaking aspen's life cycle, its role in the ecosystem, and the threats it faces. *Grades 3 and up; nonfiction.*

Squirrels

Gooseberry Park by Cynthia Rylant (Boston: Sandpiper, 2007). Kona, a Labrador retriever, and Stumpy, a squirrel, meet one day in Gooseberry Park, and they become fast friends. When Stumpy needs help, Kona comes to the rescue, and shows what a true and loyal friend he is. *Grades 3–5; fiction.*

Squirrels in the School by Ben M. Baglio (New York: Scholastic, 2000). When Mandy and James find a family of squirrels nesting inside the school, they have to work together to keep the squirrels safe from school officials who are eager to get rid of them. *Grades 3–5; fiction.*

Turkeys

Wild Turkeys by Dorothy Hinshaw Patent (Minneapolis: Lerner, 1999). This book introduces kids to the life cycle and behavior of turkeys, and also explores some of the similarities and differences between wild turkeys and farm turkeys. *Grades 2–4; nonfiction.*

Venus Flytraps

Hungry Plants by Mary Batten (New York: Random House, 2000). This book gives kids an up-close look at Venus flytraps and other carnivorous plants. *Grades 2–3; nonfiction.*

Wolves

Julie of the Wolves by Jean Craighead George (Carmel, CA: Hampton-Brown, 1972). Miyax lives in a small Eskimo village—until her life there becomes dangerous and she runs away. Instead of fleeing to safety, however, Miyax finds herself wandering in the Alaskan wilderness. In her struggle for survival she joins a pack of wolves, becoming one of their wild family. When she finally reaches civilization, Miyax longs for her role as Julie of the wolves. *Grades 4 and up; fiction.*

White Fang by Jack London (New York: The Macmillan Company, 1906). Set during the Klondike Gold Rush at the end of the nineteenth century, *White Fang* is narrated by a wolf dog as he transforms from wild animal to domesticated pet. Readers will gain insight into the world of wolves and how they might view humans. *Grades 5 and up; fiction.*

Miscellaneous

125 True Stories of Amazing Animals: Inspiring Tales of Animal Friendship and Four-Legged Heroes, Plus Crazy Animal Antics by National Geographic Kids (Washington, DC: National Geographic Children's Books, 2012). This book is packed with inspiring, hilarious, and touching stories about incredible animals, including a sea otter that kayaks, a bear that stole a family's car, and a cat that called 911 to save its owner. Kids will also get to read true stories of unlikely animal friendships and learn facts about each different animal. *Grades 3 and up; nonfiction.*

Animal Heroes: True Rescue Stories by Sandra Markle (Minneapolis: Millbrook Press, 2008). Included in this collection of true animal stories are accounts of a guide dog that saves her blind owner on 9/11, a group of dolphins that saves swimmers from a shark attack, and a cat that saves its family from carbon monoxide poisoning. *Grades 4–7; nonfiction.*

Dog Finds Lost Dolphins, and More True Stories of Amazing Animal Heroes by Elizabeth Carney (Washington, DC: National Geographic Children's Books, 2012). Cloud is a special black Lab—the only dog certified to sniff out stranded dolphins, some that are more than a mile away from her

super sniffer. Cloud often waits on the dock for the dolphins to emerge from the water and give her a kiss. This book also includes two other stories about amazing animals. *Grades 2 and up; nonfiction.*

Owen & Mzee: The True Story of a Remarkable Friendship by Isabella Hatkoff, Craig Hatkoff, and Dr. Paula Kahumbu (New York: Scholastic Press, 2006). Owen, a baby hippo, was stranded after the 2004 tsunami and rescued by villagers in Kenya. He soon forged an unbreakable bond with a 130-year-old giant tortoise, Mzee, and the two can be seen swimming, eating, and playing together all over the preserve they call home. *Grades K–5; nonfiction.*

Character Education Organizations and Websites

Character Education Partnership (CEP)

www.character.org

A nonprofit organization dedicated to promoting character education at all grade levels. The website contains downloadable publications, lesson plans, a character education blog, and a substantive list of resources.

Educators for Social Responsibility (ESR)

www.esrnational.org

A national nonprofit organization that works with educators to advocate practices such as social-emotional learning, character development, conflict resolution, diversity education, civic engagement, and more. The website contains lesson plans, activities, articles, and links for teachers of all grades.

GoodCharacter.com

www.goodcharacter.com

Recommended by the Parents' Choice Foundation, this website contains resources for character development and service learning. Includes articles, tips, teaching guides, lesson plans, and resource lists.

Josephson Institute/Character Counts!

www.charactercounts.org

Josephson Institute develops and delivers services and materials to increase ethical commitment, competence, and practice in all segments of society.

Learning Peace

www.learningpeace.com

This site helps educators, parents, and other adults create more peace in schools, homes, and communities by teaching children conflict resolution, anger management, anti-bullying, and character building.

Search Institute

www.search-institute.org

Through dynamic research and analysis, this independent nonprofit organization works to promote healthy, active, and content young people and communities through asset building.

Teaching Tolerance

www.tolerance.org

A national education project of the Southern Poverty Law Center, dedicated to helping teachers foster respect and understanding in the classroom. The website contains resources for educators, parents, teens, and kids.

Youth Frontiers

www.youthfrontiers.org

Youth Frontiers is a nonprofit, nonpartisan organization that partners with schools to build cultures of respect where students thrive socially, emotionally, and academically. Its vision is to change the way kids treat each other in every hallway, lunch line, and classroom of every school in America.

References

Angier, Natalie. "Pigs Prove to Be Smart, if Not Vain." *The New York Times*. Retrieved June 13, 2012, from www.nytimes.com/2009/11/10/science/10angier.html.

Anthony, Lawrence. *The Elephant Whisperer: My Life with the Herd in the African Wild*. New York: Thomas Dunne Books, 2009.

Athan, Mattie Sue. *Guide to Companion Parrot Behavior*. New York: Barron's Educational Series, 2010.

Bradshaw, John. *Dog Sense: How the New Science of Dog Behavior Can Make You a Better Friend to Your Pet*. New York: Basic Books, 2011.

Brooks, Steve. *Dragonflies*. Washington, DC: Smithsonian Books, 2003.

Brusca, Richard C., and Brusca, Gary J. *Invertebrates*. Sunderland, MA: Sinauer Associates, 2003.

Chen, Z., Sanchez, R., and Campbell, T. "From Beyond to Within Their Grasp: Analogical Problem Solving in 10- and 13-Month-Olds." *Developmental Psychology 33* (1997), 790–801.

The Cornell Lab of Ornithology. www.birds.cornell.edu.

D'Amato, Peter. *The Savage Garden: Cultivating Carnivorous Plants*. Berkeley, CA: Ten Speed Press, 1998.

Davies, Hazel, and Butler, Carol A. *Do Butterflies Bite? Fascinating Answers to Questions About Butterflies and Moths*. New Brunswick, NJ: Rutgers University Press, 2008.

Davis, Karen. *More than a Meal: The Turkey in History, Myth, and Reality*. New York: Lantern Books, 2001.

Dobbs, David. "Do Animals Feel Empathy?" *ScientificAmerican.com*. Retrieved June 13, 2012, from www.scientificamerican.com/blog/post.cfm?id=do-animals-feel-empathy.

Dunlop, Colin, and King, Nancy. *Cephalopods: Octopuses and Cuttlefish for the Home Aquarium*. Neptune City, NJ: TFH Publications, 2009.

Farrelly, David. *The Book of Bamboo: A Comprehensive Guide to This Remarkable Plant, Its Uses, and Its History*. San Francisco: Sierra Club Books, 1984.

Goodall, Jane. *My Life with the Chimpanzees*. New York: Pocket Books, 1996.

Goswami, U., and Brown, A.L. "Higher-Order Structure and Relational Reasoning: Contrasting Analogical and Thematic Relations." *Cognition 36* (1990), 207–226.

Grant, M. & Mitton, J. "Case Study: The Glorious, Golden, and Gigantic Quaking Aspen." *Nature Education Knowledge*, 1(8):40 (2010).

Holland, Jennifer. *Unlikely Friendships: 47 Remarkable Stories from the Animal Kingdom*. New York: Workman Publishing, 2011.

Hollenhorst, John. "Central Utah's Pando, World's Largest Living Thing, Is Threatened, Scientists Say." *Deseret News*. Retrieved June 13, 2012, from www.deseretnews.com/article/700071982/Central-Utahs-Pando-worlds-largest-living-thing-is-threatened-scientists-say.html.

Horowitz, Alexandra. *Inside of a Dog: What Dogs See, Smell, and Know*. New York: Scribner, 2009.

The Humane Society of the United States. www.humanesociety.org.

Hutto, Joe. *Illumination in the Flatwoods: A Season Living Among the Wild Turkey*. New York: Lyons Press, 2006.

International Oleander Society. oleander.org.

Jonsson, Patrik. "Close Encounters of the Fluttering Kind: A Rise in Bird Attacks." *The Christian Science Monitor*. Retrieved June 13, 2012, from www.csmonitor.com/2005/0610/p01s03-usgn.html.

Krakovsky, Marina. "Chimps Show Altruistic Streak." *Discover Magazine* (January 2008).

Lanner, Ronald M. *The Bristlecone Book: A Natural History of the World's Oldest Trees.* Missoula, MT: Mountain Press Publishing Co., 2007.

Lassen, Niels A., Ingvar, David H., and Skinhoj, Erik. "Brain Function and Blood Flow." *Scientific American* (Oct. 1978), 62–71.

Lemonick, Michael D., and Hawthorne, Peter. "Young, Single, and Out of Control." *Time* Magazine. Retrieved June 13, 2012, from www.time.com/time/magazine/article/0,9171,987172,00.html.

Lynch, Wayne. *Penguins of the World.* Buffalo, NY: Firefly Books, 2007.

Marzluff, John, and Angell, Tony. *Gifts of the Crow: How Perception, Emotion, and Thought Allow Smart Birds to Behave Like Humans.* New York: Free Press, 2012.

Masson, Jeffrey Moussaieff, and McCarthy, Susan. *When Elephants Weep: The Emotional Lives of Animals.* New York: Bantam Doubleday Dell Publishing Group, 1995.

Mydans, Seth. "Talking to Fireflies Before Their Flash Disappears." *The New York Times.* Retrieved June 13, 2012, from www.nytimes.com/2008/12/11/world/asia/11fireflies.html.

National Geographic. www.nationalgeographic.com.

National Oceanic and Atmospheric Administration: Ocean Service. oceanservice.noaa.gov.

National Park Service. www.nps.gov.

NOVA. "Kings of Camouflage." *NOVA.* Retrieved June 13, 2012, from www.pbs.org/wgbh/nova/nature/kings-of-camouflage.html.

Pepperperg, Irene. *Alex and Me: How a Scientist and a Parrot Discovered a Hidden World of Animal Intelligence—and Formed a Deep Bond in the Process.* New York: HarperCollins, 2008.

Powell, Joanna. "Hero Pet of the Year." *Reader's Digest.* Retrieved June 13, 2012, from www.rd.com/advice/pets/hero-pet-of-the-year.

Pryor, Karen. *On Behavior: Essays and Research.* North Bend, WA: Sunshine Books, 1995.

Raffaele, Paul. *Among the Great Apes: Adventures on the Trail of Our Closest Relatives.* New York: Smithsonian Books, 2010.

Roach, John. "Moths Elude Spiders by Mimicking Them, Study Says." *National Geographic News.* Retrieved June 13, 2012, from news.nationalgeographic.com/news/2007/02/070214-moths-mimic.html.

Rota, Jadranka, and Wagner, David L. "Predator Mimicry: Metalmark Moths Mimic Their Jumping Spider Predators." *PLoS ONE.* Retrieved June 13, 2012, from www.plosone.org/article/info:doi%2F10.1371%2Fjournal.pone.0000045.

Sanchez, Anita. *The Teeth of the Lion: The Story of the Beloved and Despised Dandelion.* Blacksburg, VA: McDonald and Woodward Publishing Company, 2006.

Savage, Candace. *Bird Brains: The Intelligence of Crows, Ravens, Magpies, and Jays.* San Francisco: Sierra Club Books, 1995.

Schorger, A.W. *The Wild Turkey: Its History and Domestication.* Norman: University of Oklahoma Press, 1966.

Siebert, Charles. "An Elephant Crackup?" *New York Times* Magazine. Retrieved June 13, 2012, from www.nytimes.com/2006/10/08/magazine/08elephant.html.

The Smithsonian. "Famous Horses." *Smithsonian.* Retrieved June 13, 2012, from www.si.edu/encyclopedia_si/nmnh/famehors.htm.

Stewart, Amy. *Wicked Plants: The Weed That Killed Lincoln's Mother and Other Botanical Atrocities.* Chapel Hill, NC: Algonquin Books, 2009.

Thorington, Richard W., and Ferrell, Katie E. *Squirrels: The Animal Answer Guide.* Baltimore: The Johns Hopkins University Press, 2006.

Time Magazine. "Top 10 Heroic Animals." Retrieved June 13, 2012, from www.time.com/time/specials/packages/article/0,28804,2059858_2059863_2060459,00.html.

Waldbauer, Gilbert. *Fireflies, Honey, and Silk.* Berkeley: University of California Press, 2009.

Walker, Matt. "Longest Insect Migration Revealed." *BBC.com.* Retrieved June 13, 2012, from news.bbc.co.uk/earth/hi/earth_news/newsid_8149000/8149714.stm.

Watson, Lyall. *The Whole Hog: Exploring the Extraordinary Potential of Pigs.* Washington, DC: Smithsonian Books, 2004.

Weaver, Janelle. "Monkeys Go Out on a Limb to Show Gratitude." *Nature: International Weekly Journal of Science.* Retrieved June 13, 2012, from www.nature.com/news/2010/100112/full/news.2010.9.html.

Yanowitz, Karen L. "Using Analogies to Improve Elementary School Students' Inferential Reasoning About Scientific Concepts." *2001 School Science and Mathematics Association Vol. 101 Issue 3* (March 2001).

Index

About the Author

A former public school teacher and gifted education teacher and coordinator, Barbara A. Lewis has received many awards for excellence in teaching, writing, and leading young people in service projects and social action. She and her students have been honored for community contributions by Presidents Ronald Reagan and George H.W. Bush and featured in the *Congressional Record,* as well as in national media outlets such as *Newsweek, Wall Street Journal, Family Circle, CBS This Morning, CBS World News,* and CNN. Barbara's books include *What Do You Stand For? For Kids: A Guide to Building Character, The Kid's Guide to Social Action,* and *Kids with Courage.* Barbara is a sought-after speaker on topics including character development, service, and social action. She has lived in Indiana, New Jersey, Switzerland, Belgium, Utah, and Poland. Barbara and her husband, Lawrence, currently reside in Park City, Utah. They have four children and ten grandchildren.

Other Great Books from Free Spirit

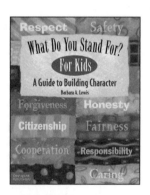

What Do You Stand For? For Kids: A Guide to Building Character
For ages 8 & up. 172 pp., softcover, 7¼" x 9"

The Kid's Guide to Service Projects
For ages 10 & up. 160 pp., softcover, 6" x 9"

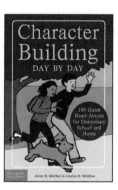

Character Building Day by Day
For educators and parents of kids in grades 3–6. 208 pp., softcover, 6" x 9"

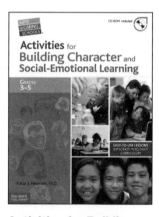

Activities for Building Character and Social-Emotional Learning: Grades 1–2
For educators, grades 1–2. 208 pp., softcover, 8½" x 11"

Interested in purchasing multiple quantities and receiving volume discounts?
Contact edsales@freespirit.com or call 1.800.735.7323 and ask for Education Sales.

Many Free Spirit authors are available for speaking engagements, workshops, and keynotes.
Contact speakers@freespirit.com or call 1.800.735.7323.

For pricing information, to place an order, or to request a free catalog, contact:

Free Spirit Publishing Inc. • 217 Fifth Avenue North • Suite 200 • Minneapolis, MN 55401-1299
toll-free 800.735.7323 • local 612.338.2068 • fax 612.337.5050 • help4kids@freespirit.com • www.freespirit.com